Advanced Introduction to the Economics of Organization

Advanced Introduction to

The Economics of Organization

RICHARD N. LANGLOIS

Professor of Economics, Head, Department of Economics, University of Connecticut, USA

Elgar Advanced Introductions

Cheltenham, UK • Northampton, MA, USA

Published by
Edward Elgar Publishing Limited
The Lypiatts
15 Lansdown Road
Cheltenham
Glos GL50 2JA
UK

Edward Elgar Publishing, Inc.
William Pratt House
9 Dewey Court
Northampton
Massachusetts 01060
USA

Authorised representative in the EU for GPSR queries only: Easy Access System Europe – Mustamäe tee 50, 10621 Tallinn, Estonia, gpsr.requests@easproject.com

A catalogue record for this book
is available from the British Library

Library of Congress Control Number: 2024952776

Printed on elemental chlorine free (ECF)
recycled paper containing 30% Post-Consumer Waste

ISBN 978 1 80392 291 1 (cased)
ISBN 978 1 80392 293 5 (paperback)
ISBN 978 1 80392 292 8 (eBook)

Printed and bound in the USA

Contents

Figures

Boxes

Preface

This book is an introduction to the Economics of Organization. On the one hand, it tries to convey, in mostly non-technical language, some of the basic ideas of a field in economics whose contours are fairly well agreed upon. On the other hand, it also tries to think about "organization" more broadly, and – as those who know my work will not be surprised to learn – it is in the end an idiosyncratic and very personal account of that field. Robert Shiller (2019) has pointed out that economics is driven by *narratives*, many of which "go viral" and influence not only the conduct of economics but often public policy. The Economics of Organization is rich with narratives, or what I call didactic fables. The book makes use of such parables as stepping stones to understanding the theories. Not incidentally, it also deconstructs many of these fables.

The book grew out of a course in the Economics of Organization that I taught at the University of Connecticut for many years. The reader may feel that the book tries to capture some of the flavor of a course, including asides and even the occasional bad joke.

The course was always formally a graduate course in the Economics Department, but in fact, it often attracted many undergraduate Honors students (for whom taking a couple of graduate courses has been a requirement) as well as graduate students from Management, Finance, Accounting, Agricultural Economics, and even Sociology. The book might well appeal to good undergraduate majors, preferably with exposure to intermediate microeconomics or the equivalent, not because it engages in much of that kind of analysis but because some grounding in standard economics is valuable to provide basic language and context to the arguments here. When I occasionally taught an undergraduate course formally titled Industrial Organization, I spent a lot of time on many of the ideas now in this book, and I can imagine an instructor using this book as a supplement in that kind of course.

The book may be most useful to students (graduate or undergraduate) in a business school program, especially Management or Strategy. A number of Management students have told me that the course was extremely helpful in studying for their qualifying exams. Indeed, the book could be used as a text or supplement in various kinds of strategy courses at many levels. I hope the book will also be useful to students in graduate programs in Economics as a supplement and counterpoint to a mathematical treatment.

In the end, however, this book is intended for any intelligent reader who wants to think about why tasks and transactions in the economy are organized the way they are.

Thanks to Bob Gibbons, Leshui He, Tom Miceli, and Bingkun Wang for useful comments. None are implicated in the result. I dedicate the book to my students, especially those who had the stamina and good grace to sit through a semester of the Economics of Organization.

1   The division of labor

"The greatest improvement in the productive powers of labour, and the greater part of the skill, dexterity, and judgment with which it is any where directed, or applied, seem to have been the effects of the division of labour" (Smith 1976 [1776], I.i.1). Thus begins Adam Smith's *Wealth of Nations*, the monumental treatise that would help crystallize economics as a distinct field of intellectual inquiry. In leading with the division of labor, Smith makes organization not only a founding concern of economics but arguably *the* founding concern of economics.

Writing at the end of the eighteenth century, Smith was witnessing a remarkable growth of trade, both domestic and international. Yet the large-scale mechanization we have come to think of as the Industrial Revolution was still in its infancy. Thus, Smith understood the growth in the extent of the market he was observing as catalyzing not primarily a technological response but rather an organizational one. In the local and small-scale economy of the European Middle Ages, production had been carried out largely through crafts production: a single artisan, sometimes with the help of apprentices and journeymen, would undertake the complete set of tasks necessary to construct an artifact, using tools specialized to each task. What Smith observed in his early-modern world was not so much a change in tools and techniques as a change in the way the entire structure of tasks was organized.

Let numbers represent tasks – the stages of production of an artifact – and let letters represent human operatives. In crafts production (Figure 1.1), each artisan separately undertakes all five tasks. This has some advantages. For one thing, the artisans can all work at their own pace. In addition, *systemic innovation* – innovation that requires simultaneous change in more than one stage of production – is relatively cheap because

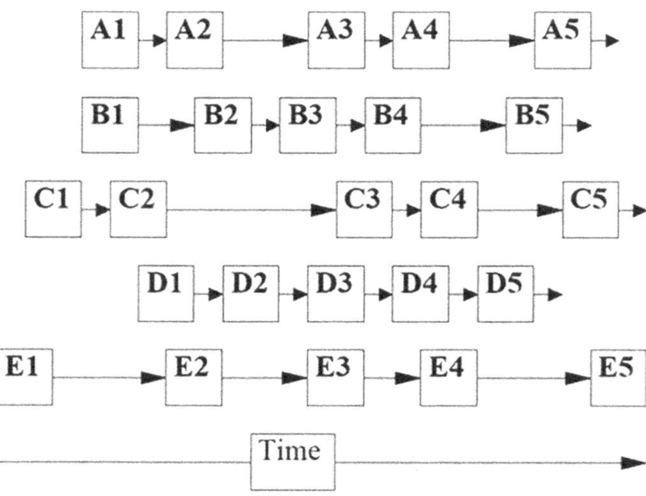

Figure 1.1   Crafts production

the artisan controls all the stages and all the interfaces between stages.[1] Indeed, systemic innovation is characteristic of crafts production. As viewers of *Antiques Roadshow* are well aware, a product made by an artisan is typically more valuable than a similar mass-produced version (all other things equal) because of its systemic variation: it is one of a kind. Notice that crafts production requires what we might call *wide* human capital. Even though different stages of production may demand substantially different sets of skills, the artisan must undertake all the tasks necessary to make the artifact and thus must master all the necessary skills.

The downside of crafts production is pretty easy to see. It doesn't scale well. At best, crafts production operates at constant returns to scale: if you want to double output, you have to double the number of artisans and the number of sets of tools. Adam Smith noticed that if the extent of the market is large enough, productivity can be increased dramatically, without changing tools or technology, simply by redesigning the assignment of tasks. Under the division of labor, each artisan specializes in only one stage of production, handing off semi-finished parts

---

[1]   The terminology of systemic versus autonomous innovation is from Teece (1986, p. 288). Robertson and Alston (1992) distinguish between *integrative* and *differentiating* innovation.

to another operative who is specialized in a different stage (Figure 1.2). Smith famously illustrates this principle with the "trifling" example of pin-making. "One man draws out the wire, another straights it, a third cuts it, a fourth points it, a fifth grinds it at the top for receiving the head; to make the head requires two or three distinct operations; to put it on, is a peculiar business, to whiten the pins is another; it is even a trade by itself to put them into the paper; and the important business of making a pin is, in this manner, divided into about eighteen distinct operations, which, in some manufactories, are all performed by distinct hands, though in others the same man will sometimes perform two or three of them" (Smith 1976 [1776], I.i.3).

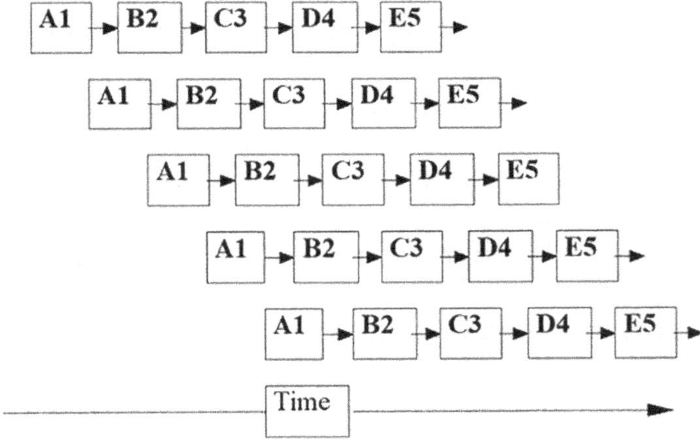

Figure 1.2   The division of labor

Box 1.1 Monsieur Prony's problem

Gaspard Riche de Prony had a serious problem. It was 1792, and the French Revolution was raging. A nobleman and graduate of the École des Ponts et Chaussées, the elite French engineering school, Prony had been charged by the National Assembly with the unenviable task of compiling, to high accuracy, extensive new tables of trigonometric functions and logarithms to suit the metric cadastral standards the Assembly wished to impose on French society.

As he walked through Paris in a near daze, contemplating his gargantuan task – and the possible penalty for failing to accomplish it – Prony stumbled into a bookstore. There he absent-mindedly thumbed through *The Wealth of Nations*. When he came to Smith's discussion of how pins were made with great efficiency using the division of labor, he suddenly glimpsed the solution to his problem. Logarithms could be manufactured just like pins.

Prony enlisted several eminent French mathematicians to devise formulas appropriate for numerical calculation. They handed their results off to a small team of run-of-the-mill mathematicians who then turned the formulas into simple algorithms. The actual numerical calculations would be performed by a large team of 60 to 80 operatives, most of whom knew no math beyond simple addition and subtraction. Indeed, in the event, the calculators came largely from the ranks of unemployed hairdressers, a group who had lost their once elaborately coiffed clients to the same Revolutionary taste for austerity and reason that had inspired Prony's commission. By 1794, the logarithm factory was producing 700 results a day (Grattan-Guinness 1990). Herbert Simon and Allen Newell (1958) went so far as to credit Prony (along with Smith and Babbage) as the inventor of the computer.

It is a bit ironic, of course, that a Frenchman had to learn about the division of labor from a Scotsman. Adam Smith almost certainly picked up the idea, along with the pin-factory example, from the French (Peaucelle and Guthrie 2011).

For a variety of reasons, in the end, the Assembly's new standards were never adopted, and little use was ever found for Prony's great achievement.

To complete an artifact using the division of labor, operatives must work as a team. They are no longer substitutes for one another but have become complements in production (Leijonhufvud 1986). To put it another way, the operatives are now wired in series rather than in parallel. This arrangement has a number of implications, both for the work experience and for the product. The time-phasing of operations now becomes important, and operatives must ultimately work at the pace of the team, not at their own pace. To facilitate the coordination between specialized operatives, both the semifinished parts and ultimately the artifact itself must become much more standardized.[2] Note also that this reorganiza-

---

[2]   The problem of coordinating among stages, including the problem of innovating across stages, implicates perhaps the most important concept

tion of production is capital saving: whereas craft artisans each needed five sets of tools, the specialized operatives now need only one set each.

Smith noted a number of advantages to this arrangement. One arises out of what we would now think of as ordinary neoclassical economies of scale. Operatives no longer waste time leisurely "sauntering" from one workstation to the next, where they would have had to set up a new set of tools. With specialization, they can spread the fixed set-up costs of their sole workstation over more units of output. Far more important to Smith, however, were the benefits of learning by doing. When operatives specialize, they get better at their jobs. Smith framed this in terms of increased "dexterity," even though he certainly understood that on-the-job learning is about far more than just simple physical dexterity.[3] Under the division of labor, operatives acquire *deep* human capital, not wide human capital.

Like David Hume, his friend and fellow philosopher of the empiricist Scottish Enlightenment, Smith thought of the human being as a *tabula rasa* upon which experience, including practice in a task, could write. In the nineteenth century, Charles Babbage would suggest that people might also come pre-loaded with different skills, or at least with different potentials for skills, which Babbage explicated in terms of David Ricardo's breakthrough idea, comparative advantage (Babbage 1846). This means that the division of labor not only improves the skills of vanilla operatives (thus perhaps helping to *create* comparative advantages), it also permits the operatives to be assigned to tasks according to their pre-existing comparative advantages. (As basketball coaches like to point out, you can't teach height.)

For Smith, specialization leads to another, even more important, form of learning by doing: innovation. When workers focus narrowly on a single task – when they become experts, in effect – they are in a better position to notice ways to improve the sequence of operations they are carrying

---

in the economics of organization – transaction costs – which we turn to in Chapter 2.

[3]   In Smith's day, the term "dexterity" had a larger meaning than it does today. In his famed dictionary, Smith's acquaintance Samuel Johnson gives the second meaning as: "Readiness of contrivance; quickness of expedient; skill of management." As Johnson makes clear in examples, "dexterity" in the eighteenth century meant something much closer to what, in Chapter 7, we will call *capabilities*.

out and the tools they are using. "Men are much more likely to discover easier and readier methods of attaining any object, when the whole attention of their minds is directed towards that single object, than when it is dissipated among a great variety of things" (Smith 1976 [1776], I.i.8). To the extent that they can appropriate the benefits of the improvements, perhaps in the form of increased leisure, specialized operatives can have a genuine incentive to innovate. Here Smith tells the amusing but wholly mythical story of how an automatic feedback mechanism was invented in the very earliest steam engines: young boys had originally been employed to open and close a valve manually, Smith claims, but, wishing to go off and play with his friends, one apocryphal boy figured out how to tie a string between parts of the mechanism so that the valve opened and closed at the right time by itself.

Note that this kind of innovation is fundamentally *autonomous* in character. It is focused on improving individual tasks or stages of production, not on altering the relationships between the stages or the overall architecture of the system.[4] Yet, for Smith, the division of labor also facilitates systemic innovation. Systemic innovation can *itself* become a specialty, pursued by "those who are called philosophers or men of speculation, whose trade it is not to do any thing, but to observe every thing; and who, upon that account, are often capable of combining together the powers of the most distant and dissimilar objects" (Smith 1976 [1776], I.i.9). With a growing extent of the market, some people will specialize in the task of invention itself. An obvious example is Smith's acquaintance and fellow Scotsman James Watt, who was dramatically improving the steam engine during the same years Smith was writing.[5] The first mature Watt steam engine was put into service with great fanfare in March 1776, precisely

---

[4]   In Chapter 9, we will discuss this as a distinction between *architectural innovation* (Henderson and Clark 1990) and *modular innovation* (Langlois and Robertson 1992).

[5]   Consider also Edmund Cartwright, trained as an Anglican minister, who not only developed the power loom, one of the key inventions in textile history, but also "developed agricultural machinery; designed fireproof building materials; made medical discoveries; contrived a crank-operated, horse-less 'centaur carriage'; and experimented with manures and potatoes as the superintendent of the Duke of Bedford's model farm" (Howes 2017, p. 10). Such specialized tinkerers and improvers were abundant in Britain during the early modern period, an efflorescence that was arguably crucial to the location of the Industrial Revolution in Britain.

one day before the publication of *The Wealth of Nations* (Marsden 2002, p. 101).

There is another source of increasing returns lurking within the division of labor. Not all stages of production will have the same rate of through-put. If one stage – stage D, for example – is a laggard or bottleneck, we could simply add another operative at stage D to take on some of the work as we expand output. But suppose stage D were in fact twice as efficient as the neighboring stages (Figure 1.3). In that case, stage D would be an "anti-bottleneck." If the extent of the market warranted two assembly lines, we could funnel both lines through the existing stage D. That means we will have doubled output without doubling our inputs, which is the definition of increasing returns to scale. As the extent of the market increases, these sources of increasing returns will continually pop up with greater fine-tuning of the production system and as existing tasks become more finely subdivided.

And here lies the source of Smith's fascination with the division of labor. Writing during a period in which Britain was a poor but developing country, he was in search of the sources of economic growth. Contrary to the doctrines of what Smith would himself be responsible for brand-ing as *mercantilism*, economic growth consists in expanding real pro-ductivity, not hoarding metallic money or inducing a favorable balance of trade. Because of the benefits of the division of labor, productivity growth depends on an increasing extent of the market. And tariffs and other mercantilist barriers to trade work to limit rather than extend the market.

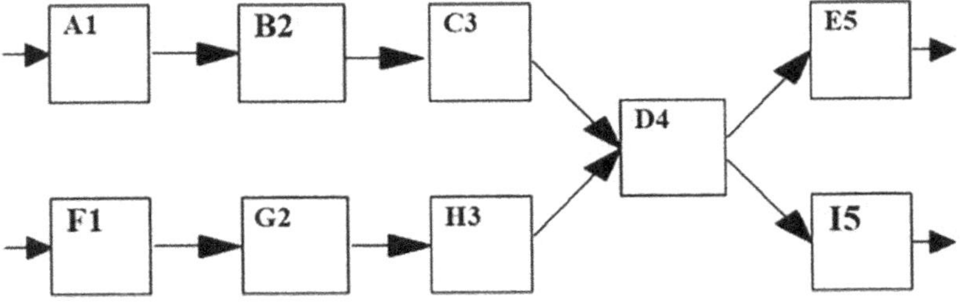

Figure 1.3   Parallel-series scale economies

Suggested readings

Richard N. Langlois, "Fission, Forking, and Fine Tuning," *Journal of Institutional Economics* **14**(6): 1049–1070 (December 2018).

Axel Leijonhufvud, "Capitalism and the Factory System," in Richard N. Langlois, ed., *Economics as a Process: Essays in the New Institutional Economics*. New York: Cambridge University Press, 1986, pp. 203–223.

John Kay, "Adam Smith and the Pin Factory," *Adam Smith Panmure House*, 16 June 2021. Available at: https://www.panmurehouse.org/perspectives/articles/adam-smith-and-the-pin-factory/.

Adam Smith, *An Enquiry into the Nature and Causes of the Wealth of Nations*. Oxford: Clarendon Press, 1976, especially Book I, Chapters 1–3.

Willy Staley, "22 Hours in Balthazar," *The New York Times Magazine*, October 17, 2013. Available at: https://www.nytimes.com/2013/10/20/magazine/22-hours-in-balthazar.html.

Coase and transaction costs

The division of labor is necessarily the beginning of any discussion of the economics of organization. But it is only the beginning. Perhaps surprisingly, the idea of the division of labor ultimately says very little by itself about what is perhaps the central question of the economics of organization: why are the stages of production sometimes coordinated through price signals in a market and sometimes coordinated within organizational structures like the business firm? In the lingo of economics: why are enterprises sometimes *vertically integrated* and sometimes not?

In presenting the division of labor, I talked about "assembly lines," possibly giving the impression that the stages of production must all be located right next to each other, maybe in a single factory building, and perhaps that all the stages have to be owned and supervised within a single firm. Smith's pins were made within "manufactories." But consider how rifles were made in Birmingham, England in the early twentieth century:

> The master gun-maker – the entrepreneur – seldom possessed a factory or workshop.... Usually he owned merely a warehouse in the gun quarter, and his function was to acquire semifinished parts and to give those out to specialized craftsmen, who undertook the assembly and finishing of the gun. He purchased material from the barrel-makers, lock-makers, sight-stampers, trigger-makers, ramrod-forgers, gun-furniture makers, and, if he were engaged in the military branch, from bayonet-forgers. All of these were independent manufacturers executing the orders of several master gun-makers. ... Once the parts had been purchased from the "material-makers," as they were called, the next task was to hand them out to a long succession of "setters-up," each of whom performed a specific operation in connection with the assembly and finishing of the gun. To name only a few, there were those who prepared the front sight and lump end of the barrels; the jiggers, who attended to the breech end; the stockers, who let in the barrel and lock and shaped the stock; the barrel-strippers, who prepared the gun for rifling and proof; the

hardeners, polishers, borers and riflers, engravers, browners, and finally the lock-freers, who adjusted the working parts (Allen 1929, pp. 56–57).

As Adam Smith would have predicted, rifle-making required a fine and extensive division of labor. Each of the rifle-making operatives pursued a "peculiar trade." Even the entrepreneur in this account represented just one of the many stages of production: the stage that marketed the rifles and arranged production. But, strikingly, the division of labor in this example was coordinated in an extremely decentralized way through market contracting among legally separate entities. Indeed, Britain had a long tradition of this kind of decentralized coordination of production. By the late Middle Ages, the manufacture of woolens, Britain's dominant industry, had moved from the urban crafts guilds to a system in which materials would be "put out" to spinners, weavers, and other specialized artisans in the countryside, who worked them up in their own cottages and were paid by the piece (Cameron and Neal 2003, p. 68). Today we call this outsourcing.

This means that to understand how the division of labor is organized, we have to think about more than just the assignment of tasks to operatives. We also have to think about the ways in which those operatives coordinate with one another and about the costs of coordination. We did this implicitly when we talked about the need for the time-phasing of activities and the imperative for standardization under the division of labor. As we will see in greater detail later, standardization is an institutional mechanism that lowers the information costs of coordinating between stages.

The problems of designing and coordinating the division of labor continued to engage engineers through the nineteenth century and into the early twentieth century, ultimately leading to what came to be called *scientific management* (Taylor 1919). Although much criticized, often rightly, scientific management would implicate many of the issues that have come to animate the modern economics of organization.[1] By contrast, mainstream economic theory in the early twentieth century was abandoning Smith's task approach and was moving instead toward a

---

[1] A major concern of Frederick Winslow Taylor was shirking – he called it "soldiering" – which we turn to in Chapter 3. Taylor usually urged a piece-rate system to create proper incentives.

highly abstract and formal price theory based around the idea of the production function.

A central preoccupation of economics has always been "value theory," also called price theory, or what we would now think of (more or less) as the theory of supply and demand. Why – everyone has famously asked – are diamonds so valuable even though they are relatively useless, whereas water is cheap even though it is fundamental to life? To answer such questions requires thinking about (among other things) costs of production, understood as the costs incurred by a representative "firm" producing these goods. But economists in the mainline tradition from Smith through Alfred Marshall would never have understood the "firm" in this theory to have been anything more than an expedient abstraction (Loasby 1976, pp. 173–192; Moss 1984). It was of limited use in understanding the organization of the complex institutional structures of actual business. As formalism took hold in the early twentieth century, however, price theory began to push aside any consideration of the firm as an institution. For Marshall, an industry was a complex ecosystem. A. C. Pigou, Marshall's successor at Cambridge, urged his followers to abandon this archaic view and to conceive of "the industry" as a simple aggregation of identical production functions, each representing a firm. By the late 1920s and early 1930s, the period G. L. S. Shackle would call the Years of High Theory, Joan Robinson could assert that what she and her colleagues were working on was no longer merely value theory: it was "the theory of the firm" (Shackle 1967, p. 11).

In fact, of course, price theory so conceived is not a theory of the firm.[2] It tells us nothing about which activities are likely to be coordinated within the firm (and thus be part of the firm's production function) and which are likely to be coordinated through the market (and thus be part of the production functions of other firms). Indeed, to the extent that coordination through the market is effective, there is no reason that each of Smith's "peculiar trades" should not always be its own firm. Why isn't *all* of production organized the way early twentieth-century rifle making was organized in Birmingham?[3]

---

[2]   "The neoclassical model of the firm is a model of production, not organization" (Barzel and Allen 2023, p. 121).

[3]   And of course, some production today *is* organized like the Birmingham rifle industry once was. For example, since the demise of the studio

In the beginning of the 1930s, this problem occurred to a young undergraduate at the London School of Economics. Ronald Coase was not a practitioner of the new formal price theory; in fact, he never took a course in economics (Coase 1988c, p. 6). But he did sample a variety of subjects, including law, accounting, and statistics, "devoting therefore very little time to each and inevitably doing no systematic reading."[4] After two years at the LSE, Coase was awarded a traveling fellowship, which allowed him to come to the United States for a year, where he proposed to investigate the motives for vertical and lateral integration. He spent most of his time visiting businesses and industrial plants. Slowly Coase's ideas and experiences began to coalesce into a theory. In 1937, he published them as "The Nature of the Firm."

As would be characteristic of Coase throughout his career, his solution to the problem was deceptively simple. "The main reason why it is profitable to establish a firm would seem to be that there is a cost of using the price mechanism" (Coase 1937, p. 390). Though he would not initially use this terminology, Coase was arguing that we must take into account *transaction costs* as well as production costs. This would not have surprised Adam Smith or Alfred Marshall. But in a world in which the firm had been stripped down to production costs alone, Coase had to create – or perhaps recreate – a whole new category of costs to sit on top of production costs.[5] Coase's crucial realization was that we cannot explain the boundaries of the firm by looking at production costs alone.[6] This is arguably the central proposition of the economics of organization.

Coase's analysis proceeds in simple Marshallian fashion: the boundary between the firm and the market will be determined at the margin. Although bringing transactions within the firm can sometimes avoid the

---

    system, the making of motion pictures has been organized in exactly this way.

[4]   In this respect, Coase exemplified Smith's "man of speculation" who is "capable of combining together the powers of the most distant and dissimilar objects" – and thus of thinking outside the box. Although he started out as a fox who knew many things, however, Coase arguably ended up a hedgehog who knew one big thing: transaction costs.

[5]   In Chapter 7, we will consider in greater depth the strangeness of this sharp dichotomy between production costs and transaction costs.

[6]   "Conclusions about the appropriate boundaries of the firm cannot be drawn simply by examining the nature of the underlying cost function" (Teece 1980, p. 225).

costs of using the price system, internal coordination also has its costs, which Coase understood in terms of ordinary diminishing returns to the fixed factor of management.[7] Thus a firm "will tend to expand until the costs of organising an extra transaction within the firm become equal to the costs of carrying out the same transaction by means of an exchange on the open market or the costs of organising in another firm" (Coase 1937, p. 395).

Box 2.1 Technology and transaction costs

In 1995, a startup called Netscape burst onto the scene with a software program for personal computers called Navigator, which allowed users to "surf" – as the practice would soon come to be called – the rapidly developing network of the Internet. Over the next five years, the Internet blossomed. By February 2000, the NASDAQ stock index, laden with Internet stocks, was almost six times higher than it had been five years earlier. At the same time, observers began to note that, often with the aid of the Internet, industry seemed to be increasingly "deverticalizing," as more and more transactions came to be carried out through the market rather than within the boundaries of firms (Langlois 2003).

In the year 2000, at the height of this early enthusiasm for the Internet, the business section of the *New York Times* featured an impressive photo of an 89-year-old Ronald Coase, walking cane in hand, on the stoop of his Chicago townhouse. (Coase would live to be 102.) The headline proclaimed: "A Nobel Prize-winning idea, conceived in the 30's, is a guide for Net business" (Tedeschi 2000). The Internet has dramatically lowered transaction costs, the article argued, which explains why firms had come to rely increasingly on interfirm agreements and alliances rather than on vertical integration.

Already by October 2000, however, the bloom was beginning to come off the rose of first-generation Internet stocks, and by 2002 the dot-com bust was complete. In a January 2002 op-ed in the *Times* business section, the noted economist Hal Varian (2002) riffed on the earlier article about Coase. Lower transaction costs do not by themselves

---

[7] In this respect, Coase's account of the costs of internal management – the costs of what is in effect central planning – is less sophisticated than that of Hayek (1945). I return to this point in Chapter 7.

imply vertical disintegration, Varian pointed out. Lower transaction costs can also benefit coordination *within* firms. Coase himself had made this point in a footnote in his 1937 paper: "It should be noted that most inventions will change both the costs of organizing and the costs of using the price mechanism. In such cases, whether the invention tends to make firms larger or smaller will depend on the relative effect on these two sets of costs. For instance, if the telephone reduces the costs of using the price mechanism more than it reduces the costs of organizing, then it will have the effect of reducing the size of the firm" (Coase 1937, p. 397n3).

In the late nineteenth and early twentieth centuries, innovations tended to lower the costs of coordination *within* bureaucracies (Yates 2000). Think about typewriters, calculating machines, punched-card readers, filing cabinets, carbon paper, and eventually large and expensive mainframe computers. Information technology always co-evolves with organizational form: in a world of large organizations, the profit opportunities facing inventors came from making existing large organizations more efficient; and the more prominent and successful those large organizations became, the more such profit opportunities sprang up.

But the Internet was not a marginal innovation. It was creative destruction. From today's perspective, it seems clear that the Internet has, in fact, done far more to facilitate decentralized than centralized coordination.

What exactly are the "costs of using the price system"? In many respects, answering that question has defined the research agenda of the economics of organization since 1937.

To Coase, the "most obvious cost of 'organising' production through the price mechanism is that of discovering what the relevant prices are" (Coase 1937, p. 390). A second type of cost is that of executing separate contracts for each of the multifold market transactions that would be necessary to coordinate some complex production activity. At first reading, then, it would appear that Coase thinks of transaction costs as akin to "frictions" in the economic system, a term that has in fact been used often to describe transaction costs.[8] Coase is concerned merely with the "ink costs" of writing contracts (Klein 1988, pp. 200, 209). But a closer reading reveals that this is not at all what Coase had in mind.

Notice that transacting parties experience costs of discovering prices and writing contracts only under circumstances of novelty and change. If nothing changes in my pattern of transacting, I won't need to keep searching, and I can continue to trade with the same partners I have always traded with. Moreover, if I'm sure nothing unexpected will happen, I can further reduce the frictional costs of contract writing by arranging a single long-term contract with each partner. "It may be desired to make a long-term contract for the supply of some article or service," Coase writes:

> Now, owing to the difficulty of forecasting, the longer the period of the contract is for the supply of the commodity or service, the less possible, and indeed, the less desirable it is for the person purchasing to specify what the other contracting party is expected to do. It may well be a matter of indifference to the person supplying the service or commodity which of several courses of action is taken, but not to the purchaser of that commodity or service. But the purchaser will not know which of these several courses he will want the supplier to take. Therefore, the service which is being provided is expressed in general terms, the exact details being left until a later date. ... The details of what the supplier is expected to do is not stated in the contract but is decided later by the purchaser. When the direction of resources (within the limits of the contract) becomes dependent on the buyer in this way, that relationship which I term a "firm" may be obtained. (Coase 1937, pp. 391–392)

The essence of the firm and its source of advantage over product markets lie in its flexibility in circumstances of change and uncertainty.

Why is a firm more flexible? By substituting an employment contract for a spot contract in output, "the buyer" can manage economic activity in real time. As Herbert Simon (1951) explained it, under an *employment relation* "the buyer" pays a wage for the right to choose which action $x \in \Omega$ the worker will perform, where Ω is the job description or set of allowable actions for which the worker contracts. The worker thus agrees ahead of time to the abstract contours of what he or she may be asked to

---

[8]   "Transaction costs are the economic equivalent of friction in physical systems" (Williamson 1985, p. 19).

do but also agrees that within those limits the wage-payer has authority to dictate a decision in any circumstances not spelled out explicitly in the original contract. Instead of buying goods or services directly on a market, a contracting party can hire a worker's time and effort and then supervise the transformation of that time and effort into goods and services.[9] Rather than being directly coordinated by Adam Smith's Invisible Hand, resources within a firm are thus allocated by what Alfred Chandler (1977) famously called the Visible Hand of management. "If a workman moves from department Y to department X," said Coase, "he does not go because of a change in relative prices, but because he is ordered to do so" (Coase 1937, p. 387).

Consider what we might call the parable of the secretary (as office workers were once called). The secretary is paid a wage for a job description of the sort Herbert Simon imagined: he must type, file, and answer the phone, but he is not responsible for making the coffee. The secretary is relatively indifferent about which of these tasks he has to undertake at any moment. But his boss is not. She sees the choice of task as crucial. One minute she may direct the secretary to stop filing and instead type an important memo; the next minute she might tell him to stop typing and instead make some important phone calls. If the future were not highly uncertain, of course, the boss and the secretary could write a detailed long-term contract in which all actions at all times were suitably priced. But in the real world, uncertainty means that contracts of this sort would be effectively impossible. Contracts are always incomplete. And this calls for a contracting structure in which one of the parties has the authority to make decisions, within specified bounds, once the uncertainty is resolved and the possibilities realized.

The idea of *incomplete contracts* is central to the economics of organization. Because contracts are necessarily incomplete, often in important ways, contracting parties must resort to *relational contracts* that permit what Oliver Williamson (1975, p. 87) called "an unprogrammed (adaptive, sequential) decision-process."[10] Perhaps we can understand the firm

---

[9] "The growth of a firm may then be viewed as the replacement of a product market by a factor market, resulting in a saving in transaction costs" (Cheung 1983, p. 3).

[10] As G. L. S. Shackle (1970, p. 160) said of money, relational contracts are a "means by which choice can be deferred until a later and better-informed time."

itself as a relational contract of this sort, an institutional framework that permits the kind of adaptive response necessary in a world of change and uncertainty. "The firm exists because it is impossible to specify all actions, even contingent actions, in advance," wrote Brian Loasby. "Incomplete specification is its essential basis: for complete specification can be handled by the market" (Loasby 1976, p. 134).

Yet although long-term contracts can be inflexible, the market in a larger sense can be highly adaptable. Armen Alchian and Harold Demsetz challenged the idea that "authority," and the flexibility that comes with it, is unique to the employment contract. "Telling an employee to type this letter rather than to file that document," they famously jibed, "is like my telling a grocer to sell me this brand of tuna rather than that brand of bread" (Alchian and Demsetz 1972, p. 777). In this sense, markets can, in fact, provide flexible responses to uncertainty, though they do so in a way different from a firm.

In the case of the firm, the buyer (the manager) adapts to change by using authority to direct resources flexibly as states of the world reveal themselves in real time. In the case of the Alchian-and-Demsetz grocery store, the buyer (the customer) can also act flexibly because the wide variety of alternative commodities available in the market permits him or her to exercise "authority" to adapt in real time. (As when your spouse calls with a changed menu after you've already begun shopping.) Effectively, a thick (spot) market for commodities plays a role similar to Simon's set Ω: You can choose tuna over bread as needed, just as you can choose typing over filing as needed, because multiple alternatives are available to you, and you have the authority to choose on the spot without negotiation.

Whether a firm is superior to markets will depend (1) on the state of actually existing markets and (2) on the nature of the adaptation problem involved. It is easy to add value over markets if markets simply don't exist. When Alchian and Demsetz walked into an Albertsons in Los Angeles in the 1970s, the shelves were full of stuff, and there was a Safeway just down the street. So it was extremely easy for them to exercise their "authority" over the grocer, that is, to design whatever pattern of final goods they wanted without having to manage directly the effort that went into producing those goods. Consider, by contrast, Charles Ingalls and family in the woods of Wisconsin in the 1860s (Wilder 1932). With no grocers to boss around, they found it much cheaper to operate as a kind of firm – to decide how to allocate their own efforts to baking bread and catching fish (though not tuna, presumably). There were perfectly good markets for bread and fish in Milwaukee, but transaction costs – transportation costs, really – made it uneconomical to extend those markets very far. To put it another way, the extent of the local market was too small to make trade in products economical, necessitating the direct management of effort.

But this is exactly why we pay secretaries by the hour rather than by the piece. The extent of the market for any particular service (like typing a specific memo at a specific time) is too small to make it worth paying the fixed set-up costs and variable measurement costs of a per-piece system.[11] In this case, however, it is uncertainty rather than the friction of wagon wheels on rutted dirt roads that makes markets costly. What an office actually produces is coordination, and the costs of failing to match the proper coordinating service (typing, filing, phone answering) with the proper moment in time are high. This raises the costs of a per-piece system, or to put it another way, raises the extent of the market for coordinating services that would be necessary for such a market to deal with the uncertainty effectively. (Modern-day apps like Uber lower transaction costs of this kind, allowing time-and-place-critical services to be priced in what is effectively a thicker market.)

The provocation issued by Alchian and Demsetz – that there is nothing special about employment contracts – had important consequences in the literature. First of all, it called into question the simple identification of the firm with an employment relation. Coase himself would eventually come to this view as well: a full understanding of the firm must take into account all the contracts the firm enters into, not just those with factors like labor (Coase 1988b, pp. 37–38). This means that we can no longer easily draw clear boundaries around "the firm." In the famous formulation of Michael Jensen and William Meckling, "most organizations are simply legal fictions which serve as a nexus for a set of contracting relationships among individuals" (Jensen and Meckling 1976, p. 310). Later chapters will try to unpack the implications of this *nexus-of-contracts* understanding of the firm and consider less agnostic alternatives.

---

[11]   In the ancient days, college students would pay by the page to have their term papers typed up. The stereotypical large corporate office of the mid-twentieth century would have a "typing pool" in which operatives – almost always women – did nothing but type, though they were typically paid a wage, not by the piece.

Suggested readings

Steven N. S. Cheung, "The Contractual Nature of the Firm," *Journal of Law and Economics* **26**(1): 1–21, April 1983.

Ronald H. Coase, "The Nature of the Firm," *Economica* (N.S.) **4**: 386–405, 1937.

Ronald H. Coase, "The Nature of the Firm: Origin, Meaning, Influence," *Journal of Law, Economics, and Organization* **4**(1): 1–47, Spring 1988.

3 Monitoring, measurement, and moral hazard

Coase's account of transaction costs, and thus his account of the firm, was all about uncertainty and costly information. Because we cannot have the highly detailed knowledge of the future necessary to write fully specified contracts, we must resort to relational contracts and, more generally, to institutional mechanisms that permit us to adapt in real time as events unfold and information becomes available. One of the consequences of contractual incompleteness is that whatever contracts we do write will retain a certain *plasticity* (Alchian and Woodward 1988). Because of costly information, it will often be difficult for the contracting parties, and for courts or other third-party enforcers, to determine whether the provisions of the contract are actually being met. There will always be a certain amount of wiggle room. As many economists quickly came to notice, this means that because of *asymmetric information*, one contracting party may be able to take advantage of the other contracting party.[1] To use Oliver Williamson's contested term, contracting parties might engage in *opportunistic behavior*.

Williamson (1975, p. 9) defined opportunism as "self-interest seeking with guile." Self-interest seeking is just the economist's usual assumption of rational behavior: people act in their own interests (sometimes broadly defined) and try to do the best they can with what they have and what they know. "Guile" goes beyond simple rationality to accuse the economic agent of dissembling and duplicity. Many critics have lashed out at this formulation on the grounds that it paints human nature in a harsh and perhaps inaccurate light (Fehr and Gächter 2000). Yet it might be worthwhile to think about the distinctive organizational problems that can arise from the potential misbehavior of contracting parties in a world of contractual plasticity.

---

[1]   Both contracting parties could simultaneously try to take advantage of each other, creating double-sided moral hazard (Bhattacharyya and Lafontaine 1995).

Yoram Barzel pointed out that problems arise even in the simplest spot transactions. "For example, determining the weight of an orange may be a low-cost, accurate operation. Yet what is weighed is seldom what is truly valued. The skin of the orange hides its pulp, making a direct measurement of the desired attributes costly. Thus the taste and the amount of juice it contains are always a bit surprising. The grower, more knowledgeable than the consumer, may gain by making the surprise an unpleasant one" (Barzel 1982, p. 27). *Measurement costs* are an important kind of transaction cost. We can explain many organizational structures and social institutions as mechanisms for reducing measurement costs.

Box 3.1 Measuring the proxy

Because measuring the (often complex) attributes of a good or service can be expensive – or even impossible – we almost always need instead to measure a *proxy*, a more easily measured variable that is correlated with what we actually want to measure. Some proxies are better than others. In the putting-out system of the early modern textile industry, the merchant clothier could easily measure the skeins of yarn and the yards of cloth the cottagers worked up. But even these were not perfect proxies, for the cottagers were adept at using starch and other techniques to make there appear to be more cloth than there really was, a practice the clothiers denounced as "embezzlement." Some have argued – wrongly in my view (Langlois 2017) – that the factory system of wage labor in centralized facilities eventually supplanted the putting-out system because it allowed direct monitoring of workers to reduce embezzlement. The costs of embezzlement were, in fact, small compared to the production-cost benefits of putting out, and it would not be until the Industrial Revolution that expensive and indivisible machinery made it economical to bring workers to a central location and pay them a wage.

The problem becomes more complicated when the good or service has multiple attributes. There may be decent proxies for some of those attributes but only bad – or non-existent – proxies for other attributes. In such cases, it may be tempting to reward the visible proxies, generating what Williamson (1985, p. 76) called *high-powered incentives*. All too often, however, this creates distortions. A famous management article ridiculed "the folly of rewarding A while hoping for B" (Kerr 1975). Bengt Holmström and Paul Milgrom (1991) modeled the problem, with the example of standardized testing in mind.

Tying teacher salaries to the success of students on standardized tests – an easily measured proxy – creates high-powered incentives. But Holmström and Milgrom found that when other, less-easily measured educational goals like curiosity and creativity are important, it may be more efficient to pay the teachers a flat wage than to tie compensation to outcomes.

This result also has implications for the choice between firm and market in production (Holmström and Milgrom 1994). If workers are paid by the piece for what are really tasks with multiple attributes, this might create the same kind of distortions as in the case of testing in schools. When there are strong complementarities among worker tasks (and among assets), it may sometimes be more efficient to pay a flat wage than to create a system of high-powered incentives.

One crucial and often hard-to-measure variable, of course, is effort. When workers are paid by the piece, they choose their own labor-leisure tradeoff. If the worker chooses leisure, he or she is simply not paid, and the worker, not the employer, bears the cost of the leisure.[2] But when the worker is paid a per-hour wage (or a per-year salary), the worker might be able to enjoy non-contracted-for leisure at the employer's expense. If there is plasticity in the wage contract – if the employer cannot cheaply monitor the activities of the worker – the worker might engage in opportunistic behavior. The worker might *shirk*.

Shirking is an example of what economists call *moral hazard*. The term famously arose from the insurance industry. As economists usually tell the story, actuaries carefully calculated the probabilities of houses catching fire and determined the insurance premia accordingly. The actuaries were outraged to discover, however, that the purchase of insurance itself changed those carefully calculated probabilities. Once insured, the homeowners had a weaker incentive to take expensive precautions

---

[2]   At least as long as the employer pays only variable costs, which was more-or-less true in the early-modern putting-out system. If the employer has high fixed costs, which were characteristic of mechanization during the Industrial Revolution, overheads must still be paid even if output is zero. In such a case, the employer does bear the costs of the worker's leisure, and the employer might well want a wage coupled with monitoring rather than a piece rate in order to better control the effort level of the worker (Langlois 2017).

against fire than had the uninsured homeowners originally measured. Some policyholders might even have had an incentive to commit arson. (Immoral behavior, sniffed the actuaries.)[3] Economists use the term more broadly to refer to any modification of behavior after a contract is signed. Moral hazard "arises in agreements in which at least one party relies on the behavior of another and information about that behavior is costly" (Alchian and Woodward 1988, p. 68).

A more focused way to understand moral hazard is within the framework of the *principal-agent problem* (Jensen and Meckling 1976). A principal-agent problem arises whenever one party (the principal), in pursuing his or her goals, delegates some activities to another person (the agent), who potentially (and very likely) has goals that diverge from those of the principal. This sort of relationship gives rise to three kinds of costs. Most obvious are the monitoring costs that the principal must incur in an (often imperfect) effort to keep tabs on the agent.[4] More subtly, the agent may also incur costs. Principals want to hire agents who are likely to do what they are asked, and so agents have an incentive to persuade the principals to hire them (or to offer them a better wage). They can do this by incurring *bonding* costs, effectively paying to alter their own incentives in a way that better aligns them with the goals of the principal. (We will explore the idea of bonding more carefully in the next chapter in the context of the hostage model.) And, finally, even after monitoring by the principal and bonding by the agent, there may still be a residual divergence between what the principal wants and what the agent does. This too is a cost.[5] Note that the divergence of goals between principals

---

[3]   In reality, when the term came into use in the nineteenth century, "moral" referred to behavioral factors as opposed to the exogenous forces of nature (Rowell and Connelly 2012). In those days, the behavioral sciences were still thought of as the "moral" sciences. The moral-hazard effect in underwriting had probably been understood since at least the seventeenth century.

[4]   Monitoring encompasses "more than just measuring or observing the behavior of the agent. It includes efforts on the part of the principal to 'control' the behavior of the agent through budget restrictions, compensation policies, operating rules, etc." (Jensen and Meckling 1976, p. 308).

[5]   It is a cost because any divergence between what the principal wants and what the agent does is not Pareto optimal. Anticipating the residual divergence, the principal will compensate the agent at a lower rate than if there were no divergence. This means that if there had been no transaction costs, the principal could have bribed the agent to work harder,

and agents can mean more than "shirking" in the narrow sense of slacking off, though it certainly can include that kind of shirking.

In one important thread of the economics of organization, institutional structures, including firms, arise as ways of minimizing the costs of the principal-agent relationship, including by lowering the costs of monitoring or by better aligning incentives. One major irony: the employment relation, which is a potential solution to Coase's coordination problem, is actually a *cause* of the principal-agent problem. Paying people a wage creates the incentive to shirk (broadly understood), since the workers no longer bear the full costs of taking leisure (broadly understood) even while they enjoy the full benefits of the leisure.

In the same famous article in which they questioned the primacy of the employment relation, Alchian and Demsetz (1972) proposed a model in which the principal-agent problem explains the existence of the firm. The key to the argument is measurement costs, in this case, the measurement costs that arise from joint production. If the boss can observe the individual marginal products of each worker, then it might be feasible to pay the workers by the piece. But if the job requires the operatives to work as a team, it may not be possible to separate out the marginal products of the team members. The monitoring problems inherent in team production will create the opportunity to shirk, say Alchian and Demsetz. The solution is to form a firm.

Imagine a group of five burly individuals who move pianos for a living.[6] They are organized as a piano-movers collective, with no hierarchy, and they split the proceeds of their efforts – a fee for each piano moved – equally. Inevitably, they must haul the heavy instruments up to high floors of buildings without suitable elevators. Even the team's commitment to worker solidarity may not be enough to overcome the bad incentives this arrangement creates. The problem, again, is that it is difficult to distinguish the individual contributions of the workers. Each worker receives the full benefits of slacking off (enjoyed as leisure) but pays only

---

   which would have made the principal better off without making the agent worse off. We will see a version of this presently in the context of the Alchian and Demsetz model.

6 This may take some willing suspension of disbelief, since in reality it's probably not that hard for movers to tell when one of their colleagues is shirking. But let's run with it.

one-fifth of the costs of slacking off (felt as reduced income because fewer pianos are moved). Because shirking is hard to detect, everybody has an incentive to shirk. In succumbing to that incentive, each team member imposes an externality on all the others, and they collectively experience what is, in effect, a tragedy of the effort commons. The resulting equilibrium is one with too much leisure and too little effort: the team moves too few pianos and makes too little money. They would all be happier in a high-effort, high-income equilibrium. (This is so for the same reason that no one benefited from the equilibrium implied in the old Soviet saying: we pretend to work, and they pretend to pay us.)

The solution, say Alchian and Demsetz, is for someone to specialize in the task of monitoring the team members. Someone should become the boss. This lowers the measurement costs of team production and helps elevate the team to the desired equilibrium.

But what is to prevent the boss from shirking the task of monitoring the workers?[7] (As the Roman poet Juvenal is supposed to have asked, *quis custodiet ipsos custodes*? Who shall watch the watchmen?) The answer is: the market. If the boss becomes the owner of what is now a capitalist piano-moving firm – if the boss becomes the *residual claimant* – the boss will have an incentive to keep workers at their desired optimal level of effort. The more pianos get moved, the more money the boss will retain after paying the wages of the workers.[8]

---

[7] "It is always possible to hire people to watch other people, but how conscientiously they will watch and report is as problematical as the original behavior that requires watching" (Sowell 1980, p. 65).

[8] In a well-functioning labor market, the boss will not be able to extract *more* effort than the workers themselves desire, since they can always quit and find another firm offering something closer to their preferred effort-wage tradeoff. Even Marx agreed with this point. Capitalists do not cheat workers in this sense. For Marx, capitalists exploit workers in the impenetrably abstruse sense that, as measured by the fallacious labor theory of value, they can extract more concrete labor from the workers than the exchange value of the abstract labor power they contracted for (Roberts and Stephenson 1973).

Box 3.2   The Guangxi boatmen

In the Alchian and Demsetz (1972) model, joint production makes it costly to measure the individual marginal products of the members of a team. This calls for the services of a specialized monitor, who can make sure the team members achieve the pay-effort equilibrium they desire. Indeed, the team members have an incentive to hire such a monitor themselves. Steven Cheung memorably illustrated this point with a tale that would become one of the great didactic fables of the economics of organization. "My own favorite example," Cheung wrote, "is riverboat pulling before the communist regime, when a large group of workers marched along the shore towing a good-sized wooden boat. The unique interest of this example is that the collaborators actually agreed to the hiring of a monitor to whip them" (Cheung 1983, p. 8).

As Cheung later revealed, this story was extracted from his own experience (Cheung 2018). When he was a child fleeing Japanese occupation in the early 1940s, he and his mother journeyed from Liuzhou to Guiping in Guangxi Province in a boat that was towed by such boatmen, who were being whipped by an overseer. Cheung's mother consoled her young son by telling him that the overseer had actually been hired by the boatmen themselves. Cheung conceded that he had no idea whether that detail was anything more than his mother's invention.

Although Cheung was the original source of this anecdote, his was not the first telling in the literature. Years earlier, John McManus (1975) recounted a similar story, transporting it to the Yangtze River, which is nowhere near Guangxi, and adding fanciful details like a female American passenger who is distressed by the whipping. Many others retold the anecdote, almost always locating it on the Yangtze and often adding embellishments of their own. According to Cheung, he had told the story to McManus as early as 1970, when, he claimed, he had cautioned against using the anecdote in print.

In the late nineteenth and early twentieth centuries, perhaps 10,000 junks plied the often-turbulent reaches of the upper Yangtze, employing between 250,000 and 400,000 boatmen, called trackers because they trudged on tracks carved along the shore. The eccentric British explorer Isabella Bird Bishop described the process of towing upstream on the Yangtze at the turn of the twentieth century. At the most powerful rapids, "several big junks, each with from 200 to 300 trackers, are all making the slowest possible progress, gongs are beaten frantically;

bells are rung; firearms are let off; the hundreds of trackers on all fours are yelling and bellowing; the overseers are vociferating like madmen, and rush wildly along the gasping and struggling lines of naked men, dancing, howling, leaping, and thrashing them with split bamboos, not much to their hurt" (Chetham 2002, p. 83).

The novelist John Hersey, who grew up in China, paints a more romantic picture of the life of the trackers. The boat in which his protagonist is traveling has its own small complement of some 40 trackers, though at a particularly difficult rapids the boat owner negotiates with the local concessionaire for 300 additional temporary pullers. A poor and forlorn lot, these local trackers nonetheless own their own harnesses, which they maintain with great care. The boat's own trackers are led by a head tracker – or "Noise Suppressor" – called Old Pebble, who motivates his charges mostly with chanties and drumbeats. Old Pebble himself needs no external motivation, the protagonist is told. "He works for work ... He loves everything he does for its own sake – everything he does on the river, that is" (Hersey 1956, p. 43).

What Alchian and Demsetz have explained, of course, is the classic owner-managed firm. The manager is disciplined precisely because she is also the owner. Yet vast amounts of economic activity in modern times flow through firms managed by people who are *not* also owners. As scholars since at least Adam Smith have recognized, a modern economy is characterized by the *separation of ownership and control.* "Being the managers rather of other people's money than of their own," said Smith about the directors of state-chartered joint-stock companies like the East India Company, "it cannot well be expected, that they should watch over it with the same anxious vigilance with which the partners in a private copartnery frequently watch over their own.... Negligence and profusion, therefore, must always prevail, more or less, in the management of the affairs of such a company" (Smith 1976 [1776], V.i.e.18). Present-day economists associate the problem of the separation of ownership from management with the work of Adolf Berle and Gardiner Means (1932), which appeared about the time Coase was visiting America.[9]

---

[9]   Contrary to what modern economists imagine, however, Berle and Means were not in fact principally concerned with agency problems between *managers* and stockholders (Lipartito and Morii 2010; Wells 2010). Like other Progressive thinkers of the time, including Louis D. Brandeis, they

In a paper that would become a foundation stone of modern finance theory, Jensen and Meckling (1976) admitted that the separation of ownership (stockholders) from control (managers) did indeed constitute a classic agency problem. But institutional arrangements have benefits as well as costs, and the benefits of separating ownership from control – the massive increase in the supply of capital made possible when investors no longer had to bundle their funds with personal supervision and thus became able to diversify their holdings – helped spur modern economic growth and vastly outweighed the agency costs of the arrangement. Moreover, argued Jensen and Meckling, there exist a variety of mechanisms, like the market for corporate control, that can help attenuate the managerial agency problem. We will return to these themes in Chapter 6.

Suggested readings

Armen Alchian and Harold Demsetz, "Production, Information Costs, and Economic Organization," *American Economic Review* **62**(5): 772–795, December 1972.

Yoram Barzel, "Measurement Costs and the Organization of Markets," *Journal of Law and Economics* **25**(1): 27–48, April 1982.

Michael C. Jensen and William H. Meckling, "Theory of the Firm: Managerial Behavior, Agency Costs and Ownership Structure," *Journal of Financial Economics* **3**: 305–360, 1976.

Richard N. Langlois, "The Institutional Approach to Economic History: Connecting the Two Strands," *Journal of Comparative Economics* **45**(1): 201–212, February 2017.

---

were worried about the separation of ownership from *control*, which they identified not primarily with managers but with large blockholders – what we would now call private equity – especially investment banks like J. P. Morgan and Company. Like other Progressive thinkers of the time, they viewed salaried management as dispassionate and omnicompetent scientific planning. "No better principle in carrying out business has yet been worked out," they wrote, "than to find able men and give them the completest latitude possible in handling the enterprise" (Berle and Means 1930, p. 69).

4   Asset specificity

Costly information and transaction costs can cause problems even for simple spot exchanges. But the problems multiply when we allow time to pass – when we move from the realm of exchange to the realm of *contract* (Alchian and Woodward 1988, p. 66). A contract is a promise parties make to each other about the future (Macneil 1974). In legal terminology, one or both parties may *rely* on the other, perhaps by making costly investments whose ultimate value will depend on the behavior of that other party. In the face of *transaction-specific investments*, one party may attempt to "hold up" the other party by threatening to pull out of the agreement if rents are not redistributed. Such holdup possibilities have implications for how the transaction will be governed. Indeed, the problem of *asset specificity*, in a variety of forms, would become central to the economics of organization.[1]

Notice, first of all, that a holdup is not ipso facto inefficient. If you hand me all your rents after I threaten a holdup, that's just a pure income transfer. The inefficiencies occur – and governance structures will be needed – if I expend resources to engineer the holdup or if you expend resources trying to prevent me from executing the holdup. Inefficiencies of this kind abound in many spheres of life (Tullock 1967). Burglar tools are a pure waste in the sense that they use up scarce resources not to create value but merely in the effort to redistribute existing wealth. Locks, guard dogs, security systems, police salaries, and tax attorneys similarly waste resources in the effort to prevent adverse wealth transfers. In some

---

[1] One might even argue that the problem became too central. Strategic holdup is a phenomenon that economists have found both rhetorically seductive and relatively amenable to mathematical modeling. As a result, many have spent their time looking for the keys to the theory of the firm under the streetlamp of asset specificity rather than exploring the darker regions of adaptation and coordination where Coase had originally dropped them.

respects, of course, we can think of the latter as a kind of transaction cost – the "costs of running the economic system"[2] (Williamson 1985, p. 8).

One way in which highly specific assets can create distortions is if the threat of rent redistribution they pose leads the participants in a transaction to underinvest in assets or to invest in the wrong kinds of assets. Imagine two parties cooperating to make and sell a gizmo that can be produced in two ways, either at high cost with an asset not specialized to the transaction or at low cost with an asset – a unique and highly complex machine, let us say – that *is* specialized to the transaction (Figure 4.1). What specialization means in this case is that the asset is valuable only in this transaction and has a negligible value outside the transaction: its next best use is as a boat anchor.[3] If they employ the specialized machine, the two parties will realize a profit of π. If they use the non-specialized machine, their profit will be only $\pi/2$. Suppose party A decides to invest in the specialized machine. Party B also brings a necessary asset to the project, but that asset is not specific to the transaction. The two parties agree to split the profit equally.

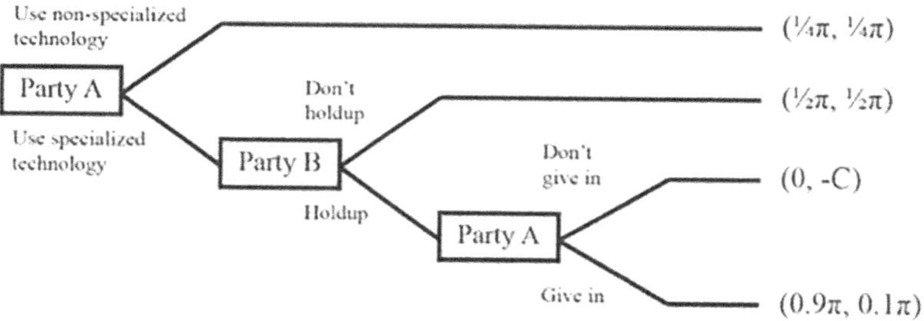

Figure 4.1   The holdup game

---

[2]   For a more careful consideration of this idea, see Allen (2000) and Langlois (2006).

[3]   Being specialized to a transaction is not the same thing as being specialized in Adam Smith's sense. There are many assets that are highly Smithian-specialized but are nonetheless available on thick markets and thus retain their value outside of particular transactions. If an asset is specialized to a transaction, it is by definition one of a kind. Yet it still might not be specialized in Smith's sense if it integrates many stages of production. We will return to the meaning of (Smithian) specialization in Chapter 8.

The problem is opportunism. A's investment in the specific asset has become a sunk cost C that A has to bear even if the project is never seen to completion. Recognizing this, party B can threaten to pull out of the deal once the investment is made unless they receive, instead of half of the profit, 90 percent of it.[4] Party A has the incentive to give in to the threat, since getting 10 percent of the profit is better than being left with nothing but an expensive boat anchor. This outcome is not inefficient: π worth of total value is created; all that's altered is the distribution of that value. But, of course, if A anticipates all this, A will be reluctant to invest in the specific technology in the first place. (And that is the equilibrium of the game in Figure 4.1, which is easy to solve by backward induction.) If A invests in the non-specific technology, there is no holdup threat, since A can recoup the full value of the investment if the project goes south. But now there *is* an inefficiency: total value now is only $\pi/2$. Notice that in this model we would never actually observe a holdup. A holdup could occur only if expectations were faulty, which means the holdup would be a surprise and thus only a pure rent transfer, not evidence of inefficiency.

The root of the problem here is that each party owns and controls his or her own asset. This means that the parties have an incentive to use their assets to transfer rents, not just to create value. Imagine instead that the two parties formed a partnership and that the partnership, not the players themselves, owned both assets. In that case, incentives are aligned because the players can no longer use the assets to attempt to extract rents from one another. Yet, at least potentially, there might be costs to this solution too. The partners in this scheme are no longer full owners of the machines they operate, which changes their incentives. Like the Alchian-and-Demsetz piano movers, they might shirk. They might even become passive owners and hire other people to run the machines, which would create a principal-agent problem. The moral here is that we cannot look at the deficiencies of one form of organization without also examining the deficiencies of the alternatives. As Robert Gibbons put it, with a slight conscious mixing of sports metaphors, we have to run the Coasean horserace among alternative organizational forms on a level playing field (Gibbons 2005, p. 203). We have to consider the costs as well

---

4   If B's asset isn't specialized to the transaction – maybe it's just an ordinary truck – A could simply go on the market and replace B's asset. For B to have a genuine threat, we have to assume that, for the duration of the project, B's asset cannot be replaced. There can be no *recontracting* until after the game is played.

as the benefits of integration. In the New Institutional Economics more broadly, this is called the method of *comparative institutional analysis*.[5]

But, you might ask, why did party A and party B not simply sign a contract? If party B failed to fulfill their side of the bargain, the court would find them in breach of contract, demanding either that B actually fulfill the agreement (the remedy of *specific performance*) or that B compensate A for the loss of sunk investment C (the remedy of *damages*).[6] With the assurances of such a contract, surely A would invest in the highly specific asset without hesitation. In simple cases, perhaps like the one in Figure 4.1, that might be possible.[7] But in general, court ordering can be costly. After all, courts are among those "costs of running the economic system." More to the point, as we saw, when coordination is complex and the future is uncertain, it is impossible to enumerate all details and foresee all contingencies in a contract. Contracts are necessarily incomplete. Courts often do not have the knowledge and technical expertise to fill in the missing contractual gaps at low cost.

It may thus be more efficient to assign the gap-filling rights – the *residual rights of control* – to one of the asset owners, who would be in a better position to maximize the value of the assets. When it is important to optimize one party's investment, then that party ought to have the residual control rights over all the assets. Note that this would solve the holdup problem, but it would also make the other party a salaried

---

[5]   The seminal paper here is that of Demsetz (1969), who excoriated the practice – still rampant today – of blithely using so-called market failures as a justification for government intervention. It is a fallacy, argued Demsetz, to compare actual markets to imagined perfect solutions. We have to compare real existing markets to real existing alternatives.

[6]   More generally, the breached-against party might be compensated with all profits foregone because of the breach, so-called *expectation damages*.

[7]   In the nineteenth-century case of *Goebel v. Linn* (47 Mich. 489, 11 N.W. 284 (1882)), a brewery contracted with an icehouse for ice at $2.00 a ton. In the days before mechanical refrigeration, breweries had to rely on icehouses, which harvested and stored winter ice from ponds and lakes, for cooling in the brewing process. Because of a warm winter, ice became scarce, and the icehouse effectively "held up" the brewery by demanding $3.50 a ton. The brewery acceded but then sued. Courts can certainly adjudicate this kind of holdup, though in this case, the court found for the icehouse on the grounds that the holdup had been caused by natural events, not opportunism (Miceli 2015).

employee or an absentee owner, and that might create a moral-hazard problem. When the investment incentives of both parties are important, a different allocation of the rights may be in order, possibly including a partnership or other form of joint ownership.

This way of approaching the problem of incomplete contracting is characteristic of what came to be called the *new property rights* literature. (We will consider the "old" property rights literature in the next chapter.) Oliver Hart and his collaborators (Grossman and Hart 1986; Hart 1988; Hart and Moore 1990) assumed that, because contracts are necessarily incomplete, specific assets are *non-contractible*, meaning that it is impossible to write contracts specifying in adequate detail how the assets are to be used once cooperation begins.[8] This implies that residual control rights are crucial, since they confer the authority to make decisions about the assets once uncertainty is resolved. Because having such authority is a way of protecting oneself against holdup by others, the allocation of residual control rights affects the incentive to invest in specific assets.

There are some striking implications of this way of modeling the problem. The new property rights literature equates the possession of the residual rights of control over an asset with the *ownership* of that asset. Although residual-control rights can be shared (among partners or even, as we will eventually see, among stockholders), they cannot be rented. A transfer of the rights of residual control is always a transfer of ownership. (If, as an apartment owner, you give your tenant full residual-control rights to the apartment, then the tenant can do anything – maybe like remodeling the apartment, trashing it, or even selling it – that you as an owner had the right to do. In renting your residual-control rights, you have really transferred ownership of the apartment.)

There is an even more striking implication: perhaps possession of the residual control rights to (nonhuman) assets – meaning ownership of (nonhuman) assets – offers a bright-line criterion for determining what lies within the firm and what lies outside of it.[9] In Hart's view, we should

---

8   More technically, the parties themselves can observe levels of investment, but the court cannot observe them.

9   Human assets can't be owned. (The United States fought a civil war over that question, resulting in the Thirteenth Amendment to the Constitution.) This means that, in the case of human assets, an ex ante transfer of assets cannot be used to deal with the holdup problem. Perhaps for this reason, many of the holdups we actually observe – like

"identify a firm with all the nonhuman assets that belong to it, assets that the firm's owners possess by virtue of being owners" (Hart 1989, p. 1766). Although this is an appealing idea, it is a controversial one, and it raises the hackles of those devoted to the nexus-of-contracts view of the firm. So complex and interesting a concept is ownership that it will receive an entire chapter of its own.

Sometimes cooperating parties can engineer solutions through *private ordering* – working things out themselves without third-party enforcement. Consider again the game in Figure 4.1. The equilibrium of the game is inefficient: at least one of the parties could be made better off without making the other worse off. Why doesn't party B simply promise party A that they won't engage in holdup if A invests in the specialized technology? The answer is that such a promise is not a *credible commitment*. Once the investment is made, party B has an incentive to renege on the promise, and A knows that. But what if B made the promise credible by changing their own incentives (Figure 4.2)? What if B provided a *hostage* – worth h to B and worth ah to A – that would be automatically forfeited in the event B reneged on the promise not to engage in holdup? (Williamson 1983b). If the hostage thus placed in jeopardy is substantial enough, B would no longer have an incentive to renege on the promise; A would know that; and A would use the more efficient specialized technology. Providing a hostage is closely related to the idea of *bonding* that we discussed in Chapter 3 in the context of the principal-agent problem.

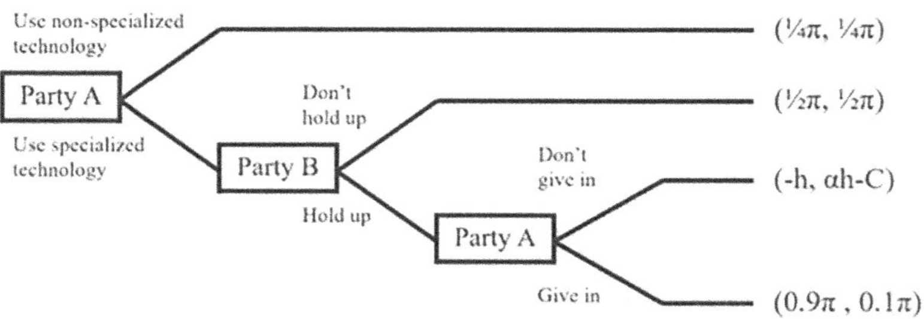

Figure 4.2   The holdup game with a hostage

star professional athletes holding out of training camp – involve human assets.

It is an example of credibly changing one's own incentives, which usually implies a cost, in order to make oneself more attractive as a trading partner.

Box 4.1 Choosing your constraints

In game theory, players make commitments (sometimes in the form of threats) in an effort to influence the behavior of other players. But game theorists understand that to be effective, those commitments have to be *credible*. The party making a commitment must actually have an incentive to carry it out as promised.

Many of these ideas were worked out in the context of the most dangerous game of all: the exchange of nuclear threats between the United States and the Soviet Union during the Cold War. Inspired by a year at the RAND Corporation, a think tank set up by the Department of Defense after World War II, Thomas Schelling produced his influential work *The Strategy of Conflict* in 1960. Schelling understood that nuclear deterrence was a modern version of the ancient practice of exchanging hostages: "the 'balance of terror' amounts to a tacit understanding backed by a total exchange of all conceivable hostages" (Schelling 1960, p. 239). He thought hard about what would make threats a credible deterrent. Simply promising to retaliate is not a credible threat: once the destruction of one's own country became inevitable, a humane leader might think it pointless and immoral to destroy the adversary's country. (I leave it as an exercise to the reader to imagine which American presidents would have pushed the button and which wouldn't.) But what if the leader had no choice? Perhaps surprisingly, Schelling concluded, it may ultimately be "a strategic advantage to relinquish certain options deliberately, or even to give up control over one's future actions and make his responses automatic" (Schelling 1960, p. 19). If your adversary understood that retaliation was out of your control, the adversary would recognize your threat as credible.

These ideas were vividly illustrated in the 1964 film *Dr. Strangelove*, Stanley Kubrick's black comedy about nuclear deterrence. It is sometimes said that Schelling was one of the inspirations for the character of Strangelove himself, an advisor on nuclear strategy who at one point cites an analysis by "the BLAND Corporation." It transpires that the Soviet Union has done precisely what Schelling had mused about: created a doomsday device that responds automatically once it detects a nuclear explosion – essentially destroying the world – and cannot be stopped by human intervention. This is a real problem for the protagonists, since an American B-52 nuclear bomber has gotten loose over Soviet territory and cannot be recalled. As Strangelove points out, however, the doomsday device was not an effective deterrent – because the Soviets had never told the Americans of its existence. ("It was to be announced at the party congress on Monday," says the Soviet ambassador with considerable embarrassment. "As you know, the premier loves surprises.")

Schelling later applied many of these ideas in a far smaller arena – the intimate contests that take place within a single mind. Very often, we are in effect two people: one of us wants to lose weight and avoid sweets, whereas our alter ego very much wants to eat that nice piece of cake. It is, Schelling thinks, a principal-agent problem in our heads, one not unlike the problem implied in the separation of ownership from control in a corporation (Schelling 1984, p. 60). The solution is the same as in nuclear deterrence: self-constraint by removing choices. Our forward-thinking self makes sure never to keep sweets in the house, so it becomes costly or impossible for our impulsive self to choose to eat them on a whim.

The most famous example of self-constraint of this sort is the tale of Ulysses and the Sirens. The goddess Circe, acting as a kind of ancient Greek Thomas Schelling, warns Ulysses about creatures called Sirens, who entice sailors to their island with an irresistible song – and then kill them. Circe tells Ulysses that if he wishes to hear the song of the Sirens safely, he must fill the ears of his crew with wax and then lash himself to the mast so that he cannot choose to visit the island. The pre-Sirens Ulysses must constrain the behavior of the post-Sirens Ulysses. "Obey my commands now," Ulysses tells the crew; "ignore the commands of that other Ulysses when he demands to be cut loose from the mast."

The point here is a general one. In economics as it is usually approached, agents maximize utility or profit within constraints set down exogenously for them by nature and social institutions. But we can also think about agents actually choosing their own constraints, at least to some extent, whether in the context of individual self-control or in the context of public choice (Buchanan 1990). In political economy, a constitution is a way for present-day voters or legislators to constrain the behavior of future voters or legislators: if the constitution asserts the right to free speech, future democratic majorities cannot install a regime of censorship, even if that would maximize the utility of those later majorities in the short run. Constitutions are essentially about *removing choices* from the democratic process.

In the economics of organization, the role of constitutional choice goes beyond the simple hostage game. As we saw, in a world of uncertainty and incomplete contracts, it is often difficult for third-party enforcers like courts to adjudicate disputes efficiently. But contracting parties can sometimes consciously choose to employ such third-party enforcers – not because the courts actually have a comparative advantage in adjudication but because the threat of outside enforcement changes the constraints the transacting parties face. "By defining performance with explicit court-enforceable contract terms, such as the quantity, quality, and price of a product that must be delivered, transactors control hold-up behavior by legally 'tying their hands' with regard to variables that can be manipulated to expropriate rents from a transacting partner" (Klein 1996, p. 456).

Virtually everyone who has written about the problem of asset specificity has considered the problem of ex ante underinvestment (or malinvestment). But, as Gibbons (2005) has pointed out, there is also a distinct strand in the literature that is concerned principally not with problems of ex ante incentive alignment but rather with problems of governing ex post rent seeking. The ex ante incentive game we just analyzed is a one-shot problem in which the parties can see clearly what is at stake. In most of reality, however, the opportunities for rent seeking aren't so clearly defined, and many of them will reveal themselves only after contracts are signed and cooperation begins. The presence of highly specific assets will make ex post rent seeking more likely and more dangerous. The cooperating parties may thus want to choose *governance structures* to help minimize adverse wealth transfers and costly haggling (Williamson 1985, p. 2). In this account, the firm arises because it is a superior governance structure for dealing with ongoing problems of haggling and rent seeking.

One of the central ideas in the asset-specificity literature is that the threat of costly ex post rent seeking increases with the size of the *appropriable quasi-rent*, the difference between the value of the specific asset within the transaction and its next best use outside of the transaction (Klein, Crawford and Alchian 1978). To the extent that vertical integration – the internalization of the entire transaction within a firm – is a potential solution to the problem of ex post rent seeking, then the larger the appropriable quasi-rent, the more likely we are to see vertical integration rather than contracting.

Indeed, Williamson (1981) proposed a simple reduced-form model in which the costs of governing transactions, and thus the boundaries of the firm, depend on nothing but the level of asset specificity (Figure 4.3). In this model, $\Delta G(A)$ is the difference in cost between governing a transaction inside the firm and governing it through the market, where A is a measure of the degree of asset specificity involved in the transaction. When asset specificity is low, ΔG will be positive because – thanks to the moral hazard of the employment relation, among other things – governing a transaction within the firm will be more costly than using the market. Bureaucracies, including those within firms, lack the *high-powered incentives* of the market. (With no asset specificity, $\Delta G = \beta$.) But as asset specificity increases, the costs of using markets will rise faster than the costs of internal organization. This, Williamson thinks, is because firms have superior mechanisms for reducing the costs of conflict over rent redistribution. Again, common ownership of assets better aligns incentives. And taking advantage of their local knowledge, managers can cheaply resolve disputes internally, perhaps by exercising fiat, without resort to the legal system. At some critical level of $A = A^*$, ΔG will turn negative. At that point, it will become cheaper to govern the transaction

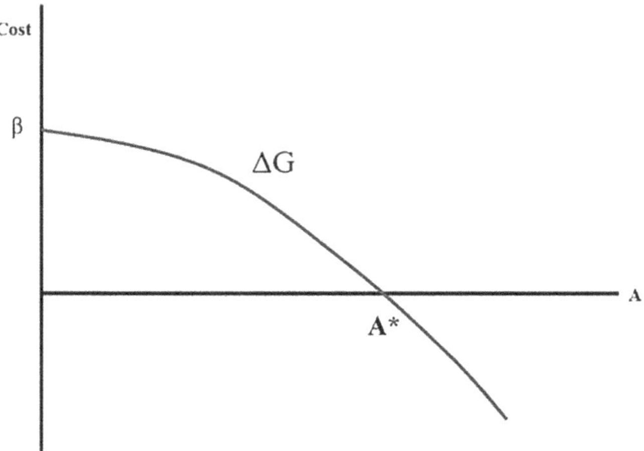

Source: Williamson (1981, p. 560), used by permission of the University of Chicago Press.

Figure 4.3   Williamson's Reduced-Form Model of Vertical Integration

within a firm. A* thus determines the boundary of the firm: we will want to govern all those transactions for which A > A* within the firm and to govern all those transactions for which A < A* using the market.[10]

Yet, the market can also manage longer-term haggling and rent seeking – once again by means of a hostage. If the game in Figure 4.1 is played repeatedly, a hostage arises naturally. Because I would profit by continuing to trade with you, I threaten my future stream of revenue if I hold you up on any particular play of the game. The discounted present value of that revenue stream is thus a hostage.[11] More generally, to preserve future custom, I would be willing to work with you to resolve conflicts over rent distribution, meaning that we may be able to achieve through market contracting many of the benefits Williamson saw in vertical integration. Only when the size of the transaction – when the size of the assets put at risk – grows too large does this hostage mechanism fail. If engaging in a one-shot holdup would afford me a more-than-comfortable life in the Cayman Islands, I may no longer care about the loss of future transactions with you. In the language of Klein and Leffler (1981), the transaction will then have been pushed outside the *self-enforcing range*.

---

[10]   Williamson also adds in the production-cost differences between the market and internal organization. Because the market can take advantage of economies of scale and scope – specialized firms in the market can probably provide you with #10 lock-washers more cheaply than you can make them yourself – adding in production-cost differences can shift *in* the boundaries of the firm. But production-cost differences will never shift *out* the boundaries of the firm. In this model, as in the economics of organization more generally, production costs alone can never explain vertical integration.

[11]   Klein and Leffler (1981) argue that when highly specific assets are at play, the cooperating parties will trade at prices above the competitive level, thus creating a stream of rents that serves as a hostage. A good example of this may have been Henry Ford's famous $5-a-day wage. Ford had been plagued by rampant absenteeism, thus leaving his many highly specific assets idle or running inefficiently. By paying well above the prevailing rate in Detroit, Ford created a stream of rents that workers would not want to lose, thus keeping them in the shop and attentive to the job. Economists call this an *efficiency wage* (Raff and Summers 1987).

Box 4.2   Fisher Body

Among the greatest – and most controversial – of all didactic fables in the economics of organization is the tale of Fisher Body.

In 1919, the General Motors Corporation bought into the Fisher Body Corporation, a large, highly integrated body maker run by no fewer than seven Fisher brothers. (The body of a car is the outer shell, including doors, fenders, etc., as contrasted with the chassis, which consists of the frame, drive train, and wheels. It was common in those days for automakers to buy their bodies from outside suppliers like Fisher.) The parties also put in place a 10-year contract making Fisher the sole supplier to GM of closed car bodies. In 1926, before the contract expired, GM bought the remaining equity in Fisher, which then became a wholly owned division of GM.

In 1978, Benjamin Klein, Robert Crawford, and Armen Alchian used the GM acquisition of Fisher Body as an illustration of the asset specificity or holdup theory of vertical integration. Because of unforeseen events, they wrote, Fisher was able to use the contract to its advantage to extract rents from GM by employing inefficiently labor-intensive methods. In this telling, Fisher also refused to locate body plants near GM assembly facilities. "By 1924, General Motors had found the Fisher contractual relationship intolerable and began negotiations for the purchase of the remaining stock in Fisher Body, culminating in a final merger agreement in 1926" (Klein, Crawford and Alchian 1978, p. 310).

Although Oliver Williamson had discussed similar issues by the early 1970s, the Klein et al. paper became identified with the asset-specificity approach. As the paper gained influence, the Fisher case grew into an omnipresent meme in the economics of organization. Over the next two decades, the Klein et al. telling of this episode would be featured in textbooks and authoritative handbooks. It would be cited by virtually every theorist proposing an asset-specificity model, none of whom had ever actually studied the history of the automotive industry. Fisher Body became "the Coasian literature's favorite example of a vertical merger" (Bolton and Scharfstein 2000, p. 234).

In 1987, Oliver Williamson and others organized a conference at Yale to celebrate the fiftieth anniversary of Coase's path-breaking 1937 paper. In discussing the history and implications of his work, Coase revealed to the conference that he had once seriously considered but then rejected the asset-specificity account as a major determinant of vertical integration (Coase 1988c). This raised some eyebrows in the audience. When the proceedings of the conference appeared, they contained a paper by Benjamin Klein that had not been presented at the conference (Klein 1988). "Coase's rejection of the opportunism analysis is based upon too simplified a view of the market contracting process," Klein scolded, "and too narrow a view of the transaction costs associated with that process" (Klein 1988, p. 200). In Klein's view, Coase's understanding of transaction costs was limited to what he derided as the "ink costs" of writing many separate contracts with suppliers.

Almost certainly because of this exchange, interest in the Fisher Body case quickened within the academic community. In the year 2000, the once uncontroversial meme suddenly exploded into a *cause célèbre*. No fewer than five papers appeared, including one by Coase himself, that challenged Klein's account. With surprising unanimity, the papers pointed to wider issues in the decision by General Motors to acquire the remaining stock of Fisher Body. Many of the papers endorsed the view of Alfred Chandler and Stephen Salsbury (1971, pp. 575–578) that GM had wanted to purchase Fisher largely to gain fuller access to the knowledge and managerial talents of the Fisher brothers. Klein responded, and there broke out a protracted – and increasingly heated – debate in print between Coase and Klein. (For a detailed recounting of the controversy by one of the participants, see Brooks [2016].)

One result of the debate is that we know a good deal more today about the history of the Fisher Body-General Motors relationship than we once did. Amid the barrage of argument, and as he more care-fully researched the history, Klein was forced to change more than once his account of which highly specific assets he believed had lain behind the threat of holdup. For example, the original Klein et al. article of 1978 mentioned the unique and expensive stamping dies that Fisher needed to make for each car model. In reality, it had been a long-standing practice in the industry for the carmakers themselves to acquire immediate ownership of such dies (Monteverde and Teece 1982) – exactly as the property-rights model would predict. Coase was scathing about Klein's treatment of the facts of the case. "It is not easy to know what to say about a situation like this," wrote the 96-year-old Nobelist. "Facts are not like clay on a potter's wheel, that can be molded to produce the desired result. They constitute the immutable material that we have to accept. What is clear in Klein's new version of the facts is that the 'classic example' of asset specific-ity leading to opportunistic behavior has completely disappeared. All that remains of the original tale is the assertion that Fisher Body held up GM. It reminds one of the Cheshire Cat in Lewis Carroll's *Alice in Wonderland,* whose body vanished, leaving only its grin behind" (Coase 2006, p. 270).

The Fisher Body episode remains highly controversial, and it is far from clear what theory has learned from it. Coase always clearly had in mind an ex ante model of holdup like that in Figure 4.2. Much of the argument between Coase and Klein centered on whether repeated interaction between the players would generate a suitable hostage. As a 21-year-old student from the London School of Economics, Coase had visited and spoken with many American businesses in 1932. He was particularly impressed with the A. O. Smith works in Milwaukee, an independent and highly successful maker of automobile frames. The Smith executives had persuaded Coase "that there were 'many contractual devices' which would avoid the risk associated with making capital investments to supply one customer, and in fact independent firms commonly made such investments" (Coase 1988c, p. 16). By contrast, Klein believed the holdup threats involved in the Fisher case were so great that they would inevitably have pushed any contractual relationship out of the self-enforcing range. More subtly, Klein did not always reason solely in terms of the ex ante model but often invoked, sometimes implicitly, the model of ex post rent seeking. Vertical integration may have been a governance structure to deal with a variety of non-specific holdup possibilities that could arise in the future in an industry requiring large capital investments.

What is clear, however, is that the Fisher Body story has lost most of its value as a didactic fable of holdup and asset specificity.

The asset-specificity or holdup theory of vertical integration would seem a far cry from the coordination theory originally espoused by Coase in 1937. But there are some significant areas of close contact.

One possible source of a holdup threat is *temporal specificity.* "Where timely performance is critical," wrote Masten, Meehan, and Snyder (1991, p. 9), "delay becomes a potentially effective strategy for exacting price concessions. Knowing that interruptions at one stage can reverberate throughout the rest of the project, an opportunistic supplier may be tempted to seek a larger share of the gains from trade by threatening to suspend performance at the last minute. Even though the skills and assets necessary to perform the task may be fairly common, the difficulty of identifying and arranging to have an alternative supplier in place on short notice introduces the prospect of strategic holdups." Now think back to the parable of the secretary in Chapter 2. It was important for one of the contracting parties (the manager) that the right activity be undertaken at the right time. Tasks were temporally specific, and the degree of specificity increased as the importance of the task and the importance of timing increased to the manager. Even though the secretary had no intention of holding the manager up, markets would never have been thick enough – at least before the advent of smartphone apps – to achieve the flexibility such temporal specificity demanded. Adding a holdup threat to this account is merely a twist to the Coasean story. Note that Coasean temporal specificity can be important even when, as in the case of the secretary, the participants are playing a repeated game and the skills involved are widely available on the market.

Suggested readings

Armen A. Alchian and Susan Woodward, "The Firm Is Dead; Long Live the Firm a Review of Oliver E. Williamson's *The Economic Institutions of Capitalism*," *Journal of Economic Literature* **26**(1): 65–79, 1988.
Robert Gibbons, "Four Formal(izable) Theories of the Firm?" *Journal of Economic Behavior & Organization* **58**(2): 200–245, 2005.
Oliver D. Hart, "An Economist's Perspective on the Theory of the Firm," *Columbia Law Review* **89**(7): 1757–1774, 1989.
Benjamin Klein, Robert G. Crawford and Armen A. Alchian, "Vertical Integration, Appropriable Rents, and the Competitive Contracting Process," *Journal of Law and Economics* **21**(2): 297–326, 1978.
Oliver E. Williamson, *The Economic Institutions of Capitalism*. New York: The Free Press, 1985, Chapters 5 and 7.

5   Property rights and organization

We have seen several stories in which firms arise because the coalescence of the rights of control – the coalescence of ownership – in the hands of a single party is more efficient than ownership dispersed among many parties. This is the essence of the so-called new property rights approach associated with the work of Grossman, Hart, and Moore: we should think about the assignment of control rights to non-human assets as a way of mitigating inefficiencies, notably including those caused by inadequate ex ante investments or by ex ante malinvestments. But this literature is in many ways a special case of an older, larger, and more general approach to thinking about organization through the lens of property rights.[1]

Perhaps unsurprisingly, this older property rights literature was inspired by Coase. In 1960, Coase published his second pathbreaking contribution, "The Problem of Social Cost" (Coase 1960), which articulated the famed "Coase Theorem": that in a world of low transaction costs, property rights will always end up in the hands of the party who values them the most, thus ensuring efficiency. Coase himself never considered this a theorem. He considered it a "bloody obvious" idea going back at least to Adam Smith (McCloskey 1997). Like the literature that blossomed from the paper, Coase was concerned with cases in which there *were* transaction costs.[2]

---

[1]   For critiques of the narrowness and formality of Grossman, Hart, and Moore's approach, see Allen and Barzel (2016), Foss and Foss (2001), and Pagano (2000). All of these authors complain that the New Property Rights literature allows transaction costs along some margins but insists on perfect information and costless enforcement along other margins, resulting, as Pagano (2000, p. 454) puts it, in "some sort of Swiss cheese where holes of incomplete contracts are open in a desert of perfectly working and costless markets."

[2]   "The world of zero transaction costs has often been described as a Coasian world. Nothing could be further from the truth. It is the world

His central focus was the phenomenon of *externalities,* uncompensated harms or benefits not transmitted through the price system.[3] As he had in 1937, Coase once again set himself against the tradition emanating from A. C. Pigou and his followers, who modeled externality in terms of a divergence between private costs and social costs. To Coase, externalities are not misalignments of disembodied costs but rather manifestations of institutional structure. And the way to understand externalities – and often the way to deal with them – is to scrutinize the underlying institutional and organizational structure, especially the structure of property rights.

Creating and maintaining a system of property rights implies a cost – a "cost of running the economic system." Sometimes, setting up a system of property rights is not worth the cost. This is why restaurants seldom bother to charge you for salt, effectively placing it in the public domain (Barzel 1997, p. 93). In modern-day lingo, we would say that there is "open access" to salt. When resources are economically valuable, however, an absence of property rights can cause real problems. It can lead to the infamous tragedy of the commons.

Consider the case of oil extraction in the United States for most of the twentieth century (Libecap and Wiggins 1984). Uniquely in the world, American law applied the rule of capture to oil production. This means that one comes to own oil only by removing it from the ground; one cannot stake a claim to an entire pool of oil beneath the surface. As a result, oil production was subject to a tragedy of the commons perfectly analogous to the one in international fisheries, which also operate on the rule of capture (by default because of the mobility of fish and the absence of enforceable international law). Just as every fisher wants to catch as many fish as possible as quickly as possible, every producer who has drilled into an underground oil field wants to suck up as much of the collective oil as possible as quickly as possible. In oil, the inefficiency occurs because pumping the fluid out of the ground too fast will ultimately yield less,

---

of modern economic theory, one which I was hoping to persuade economists to leave" (Coase 1988a, p. 174).

[3] Not all harms are externalities. If I set up next door to you and produce a product so good it puts you out of business, I harm you *through* the price system, not outside of it. The harm I inflict would be a "pecuniary" externality, which is not a real or "technological" externality. Far from reflecting an inefficiency, a pecuniary externality is the Coase Theorem in action.

sometimes considerably less, leaving much valuable oil under the ground that can then be removed only at much higher cost. In effect, each driller imposes an externality on all the other drillers.

The problem of oil extraction called for an organizational solution. A single producer might have been permitted to own an entire pool; alternatively, one owner might have operated the entire field but compensated the other owners according to a formula, a practice called unitization. Both alternatives would have created the incentive to try to maximize the net present value of the oil in the ground and to pump at a slower, more nearly optimal rate. Because of the large number of drillers and the uncertainty surrounding the value and the geological characteristics of fields, however, the transaction costs of writing unitization contracts were extremely high. In the end, American political economy settled on the second-best regulatory solution of "prorationing," which capped total output but did not enforce genuine unitization.[4]

Box 5.1   Institutional innovation

One way to interpret the Coase theorem is that whenever transaction costs are low enough, individual actors will have an incentive to eliminate inefficiencies through trade by moving resources into the hands of those who value them the most. Coase cited an example from an old English legal case: a physician had installed his consulting room against a wall behind which a confectioner was using loud machinery to make candy. This seems like an externality: the noise of the confectioner interfered with the ability of the physician to use his stethoscope. But, Coase pointed out, since it was relatively easy for the two parties to get together and bargain, why not just assign the right to either one of them (maybe even in a de facto way by doing nothing) and let them hash it out? The one whose use of the facility produced the most value should end up with the right, or the two might formulate a mitigation strategy.

Harold Demsetz (1967) quickly generalized this idea. If transaction costs are low enough, he argued, individual actors will have an incentive to bring *institutions themselves* into being in order to resolve

---

[4]   Ironically, the only genuinely unitized field in the 1920s was the Teapot Dome oil reserve, which gave its name to a famous political scandal (Libecap 1984).

inefficiencies. As we saw in examples like oil extraction or fisheries, a tragedy of the commons occurs when institutions fail to align incentives and the resource is overused. Elinor Ostrom (2015) showed that, in an astonishing variety of situations, small face-to-face groups have been able to formulate rules to govern the commons. But when there are many anonymous claimants, it makes sense to create property rights over the untapped resource. As the residual claimant, an owner would then have the incentive to exclude others in a way that maximized the present value of the resource and avoided overuse. Demsetz suggested that, since there is value to be extracted from creating ownership institutions in these situations, individual actors would have an incentive to create the institutions endogenously.

His example was the market for beaver pelts in early-modern North America. The Innu are a Cree-speaking people inhabiting what is today Labrador and eastern Québec. When French Jesuits first came into contact with them in the seventeenth century, they noted that the nomadic Innu, whom the French called the Montagnais (mountain people), appeared to treat resources as common property and had no private rights over the game they hunted. This was clearly because the human population was small compared with the resource base and, as in the case of the restaurant salt, it did not pay to establish complex rules of use let alone establish property rights. All of that changed with the arrival of European traders. Beaver fur had become all the rage in the making of the most fashionable hats of the Old World, and the traders began paying the local inhabitants to supply more and more beaver pelts. Suddenly, the demand curve for beaver shifted out radically, and a tragedy of the commons became a threat. Citing anthropological evidence, Demsetz argued that by the early eighteenth century the Innu (and other groups as well, both in the Northeast and the Pacific Northwest) had begun to mark off territory and exclude others in order to manage the beaver resource. Property rights had emerged endogenously. (As was common in groups living perilously close to subsistence, the natives of North America practiced a kind of Good Samaritan ethic: a starving outsider could kill and eat another's beaver – so long as he left the fur and tail.)

Modern-day scholars understand that contrary to what was long believed – and what is still popularly believed – Native Americans possessed well-developed notions of territorial sovereignty, at the levels of both the tribe and the kinship group. Moreover, the native peoples often recognized individual property rights. Although these may not have made sense in thinly populated Labrador, individual property rights were the norm in the somewhat warmer climate of New England, where the inhabitants practiced agriculture as well as hunting and gathering. Although many (though by no means all) Europeans argued that the absence of property rights in the European sense justified the taking of native land, in fact, the colonial Massachusetts courts recognized indigenous rights of private property when they saw them (Cronon 1983, p. 63). These rights took the form of residual claims (usufruct rights) to the produce of specific plots of land, which were typically cultivated, and thus "owned," by women. In many respects, the system of individual land rights in native New England (and other parts of North America) bore a striking resemblance to the system of land rights the Europeans themselves had employed only a few centuries earlier in what was called the open-field system (Shoemaker 2004, p. 20). The main difference between the two systems was that the Native Americans practiced slash-and-burn agriculture, moving to new land when the soil became exhausted, whereas the medieval Europeans, facing a higher relative price of land, invented a system of crop rotation in which fields were left fallow in cycles to restore fertility. In both cases, however, individuals owned the usufruct of specific plots, and those rights could be and were often traded, even though the rights would disappear when the specific field was no longer in cultivation. At the same time, other aspects of production (and village life) were managed by layers of rules like those described by Elinor Ostrom (Langlois 2017). Although the principal modern concept of unencumbered ownership, called ownership in fee simple, had a long history in England, it did not become the norm until the enclosure movement, which took off in earnest after the Malthusian crisis (and the Black Death) of the fourteenth century unraveled the complex structure of the open-field system.

What about the newly created rights in beaver in Labrador? In the end, they proved fragile and powerless against the European demand for beaver pelts. As had already happened in Russia and the European north, the stock of beaver in the entire Hudson's Bay watershed became depleted. By 1821, the Hudson's Bay Company was forced to suspend fur trading at most of its posts (Carlos and Lewis 2010, p. 12).

This does not mean that Demsetz's insight about endogenous institutional change is wrong. But it does suggest that the process is often far more complicated. Vernon Ruttan and Yujiro Hayami (1984) proposed a more sophisticated theory of institutional innovation, arguing that we must examine in detail not only the demand for innovation – which would include the Demsetzian efficiency rents to be had – but also the *supply* of institutional change, which means thinking about political processes and associated transaction costs. Very often, efficiency gains go unclaimed because of the high costs of political change. Why do so many countries of the world remain poor when governments could make their citizens better off by adopting the kinds of institutions that demonstrably created wealth elsewhere on the globe? Unhappily, there is no *political* Coase theorem (Acemoglu 2003).

Just as organization can be a solution to the problem of too-weak property rights, organization can also be a solution to the problem of too-strong property rights. This is, in effect, the message of the asset-specificity approach to the firm. When assets are highly specific to a transaction, individual asset owners may have an incentive to exercise their property rights – their veto power – by holding up the transaction or otherwise haggling for higher rents. In many cases, such as when players renege on contracts, the rights exercised are de facto ones, not de jure ones: the player who reneges may well be in violation of legal obligations but can exercise authority over the asset all the same. Here again, collective action might be able to solve the problem. If the parties pooled their rights into a partnership or corporation, or if one party bought out the others, the players would lose their power to hold one another up.

If we are to run the Coasean horse race on a level playing field, however, we have to consider the costs as well as the benefits of an organizational solution. We have already seen that by transforming owners into employees, organizations can fall prey to problems of moral hazard. But complex organizations may generate costs of another kind as well. Because monitoring is expensive and imperfect, employees (or even divisions or subunits within a corporation) can often possess de facto property rights that give them the ability to behave in ways or to deploy corporate assets in ways that generate private rents at the expense of efficiency. Sometimes the monitors themselves can be the problem: the threat of uninvited interference from the head office – what Williamson (1985, p. 142) called *selective intervention* – can distort incentives on the ground.[5] More generally, the employees or subunits of the organization can inefficiently expend resources to transfer rents rather than to create value, in

---

5   "The authority to intervene inevitably implies the authority to intervene inefficiently" (Milgrom and Roberts 1990, p. 72).

precisely the ways theorists of public choice have long believed political agents can seek rents in the public sphere.[6] This may even mean holdup threats within the very organizations that were imagined to be the solution to problems of private holdup threats.[7] Milgrom and Roberts (1990) call the costs of this kind of rent-seeking behavior *influence costs*.

One way to make sense of the tradeoffs here is to think not merely about the existence of rights but also about the rules for enforcing rights. In what is probably the second most important paper in the literature of law and economics – after Coase's 1960 paper, which effectively created the field – Guido Calabresi and Douglas Melamed (1972) proposed that there are two distinct kinds of rules for enforcing rights: *property rules* and *liability rules*. Under a property rule, someone who wishes to transgress someone else's property right must first obtain permission, normally by compensating the rights holder to his or her satisfaction. The world of the property rule is the world of the Coase theorem, the world of the new property rights literature. Trade in rights takes place ex ante, and ideally, the rights move into the hands of those who value them the most. By contrast, under the liability rule, parties who wish to violate a property right may do so without permission, so long as they pay appropriate compensation ex post. In the most famous example, the Fifth Amendment of the U.S. Constitution permits the government to take private property for public use so long as it pays "just compensation."

Clearly, in a world of low transaction costs, the property rule is preferable, as it allows those with the most knowledge and the best incentives to make decisions about resource allocation. But, for many of the reasons we have already seen, transacting ex ante may be costly. A government attempting to assemble land for a public project may face a holdup (or holdout) problem not unlike those feared in the literature of asset specificity (Miceli and Segerson 2012). It might thus be more efficient to place decision-making in the hands of a third-party enforcer, even if that third party has poorer information about the uses and value of the rights than do the players themselves. In the land-acquisition case, the third party is typically a court, which adjudicates any disputes ex post and assigns compensation as best it can, guided by legal precedent. But a firm is also a

---

[6]   For an introduction to the theory of public choice, see Holcombe (2016).

[7]   Indeed, Robert Freeland (2000) argued that the real Fisher Body-GM holdup problem was that the Fisher brothers successfully held up GM *after* they became employees.

third party that effectively determines rights and compensation ex post. To put it another way, a court is a kind of firm, one both temporary and (in principle) impartial, which is called in to adjudicate when the process of voluntary ex ante transaction breaks down (Miceli 2015). Like a court, a firm is a liability-rule mechanism.

Box 5.2   The anticommons

A tragedy of the commons occurs when too many people have the right to use a good that is rival in consumption and no one has exclusion rights. As we saw, this leads to inefficiency as rents are dissipated by overuse of the resource. But the opposite problem can also happen. If too many people have exclusion rights – if too many people have veto power – an analogous problem can occur as rents are inefficiently minimized by *underuse*. This is the tragedy of the *anticommons* (Heller 1998; Heller and Eisenberg 1998).

James Buchanan and Yong Yoon (2000) illustrated the problem with a simple model. Think of a parking lot near a touristy village somewhere. The lot is too small to accommodate all open-access demand. If there are no exclusion rights, there will be a tragedy of the commons – an all-too-common tragedy where parking is concerned (Shoup 2005) – and rents will be dissipated as people drive around futilely looking for a parking spot. If there is a single owner, by contrast, he or she will charge a fee that maximizes the total rents of the parking lot. This is efficient. But suppose instead that there are *two* "owners," and would-be parkers must purchase both a green ticket from owner A and a red ticket from owner B. (The two can't collude or alienate their vetoes.) This will lead to less-than-optimal utilization of the resource, since the two owners together will charge a fee that is higher than the optimal charge. Using a simple game-theoretical model, Buchanan and Yoon show that as the number of "owners" – the number of vetoes – gets larger, the rents from the lot will approach zero. Too many owners is inefficient in exactly the same way as too few owners.

One of the areas in which the anticommons has been feared is intellectual property rights (Heller and Eisenberg 1998). In the case of a complex systems product – one made out of many potentially patented components – the owners of intellectual property might act like the parking-lot ticket sellers, reducing use of the technology and slowing innovation by threatening vetoes and demanding compensation. Most historical cases are controversial, including early cases involving the airplane (an IP battle between the Wright brothers and the inventor Glenn Curtiss) and the radio. In principle, a patent anticommons can be solved by a patent pool, which is in effect a kind of Coasean bargain among holders of vetoes. In many historic cases, the government has becomebecame involved, with more controversial results. The aircraft patent wars ended during World War I when the military imposed a patent-sharing agreement that favored government procurement (Katznelson and Howells 2014). Patent conflict in radio was also ended after World War I, in this case by the creation of a new entity, the Radio Corporation of America, which the navy had instigated as a "national champion" to keep radio technology out of foreign – meaning British – hands (Aitken 1985). The new entity was initially co-owned by patent-holders General Electric, AT&T, Westinghouse, and United Fruit (which had developed radio technology to communicate with its far-flung plantations and ships). It is far from clear that this spurred innovation, as RCA engaged in package licensing, meaning that a would-be radio maker had to pay for all the patents RCA held even if it wasn't using all of them. This policy arguably impeded innovation in radio components (Graham 1986, p. 41).

A less controversial arena in which the anticommons wreaks havoc is in developing and post-communist countries (Heller 1998), where bureaucratic players hold vetoes they can exchange for bribes. In 1999, my late friend and colleague Mwangi S. (Samson) Kimenyi was tabbed to run a new think tank in Nairobi to advise the Kenyan government on economic policy (KIPPRA 2022). At some point during his tenure as executive director, Samson returned to give a department talk about his experience. One of my colleagues asked him: "So, Samson, what was your greatest success at the Institute?" He thought for a minute. "Our greatest success was probably convincing the Kenyan government to reduce the number of permits required to start a new business from 140 to four."

Suggested readings

James M. Buchanan and Yong J. Yoon, "Symmetric Tragedies: Commons and Anticommons," *The Journal of Law and Economics* **43**(1): 1–13, 2000.

Guido Calabresi and A. Douglas Melamed, "Property Rules, Liability Rules, and Inalienability: One View of the Cathedral," *Harvard Law Review* **85**(6): 1089–1128, 1972.

Ronald H. Coase, "The Problem of Social Cost," *The Journal of Law and Economics* **3**: 1–44, 1960.

Harold Demsetz, "Toward a Theory of Property Rights," *The American Economic Review* **57**(2): 347–359, 1967.

Harold Demsetz, "Information and Efficiency: Another Viewpoint," *Journal of Law and Economics* **12**(1): 1–22, 1969.

6 Ownership, complex contracting, and hybrids

We began by framing the central problem of the economics of organization in rather stark terms: why are some transactions undertaken via market exchange and some transactions undertaken within the boundaries of the firm? Implicitly, and often explicitly, we have understood "the market" to consist of price-mediated spot exchanges between anonymous buyers and sellers and "the firm" to consist of direction exercised by a "boss" who is, in the simplest case, an owner-manager. This characterization is not wrong; indeed, it is foundational. But if we crank up the magnification, we will discover that both firms and markets are far more complicated entities.

First of all, as we have already seen, transactions in markets need not be anonymous spot exchanges but can be contracts, promises by one set of specific named persons to another set of specific named persons, extending over time. In one reading, as we also saw, the firm is nothing more than a "nexus" of such contracts. The firm is a place where many contracts come together, but in the end, it is not defined by any particular contract, including the employment contract. This book has been subtly dissenting from that view, insisting instead that one relationship among parties is central to the meaning of a firm yet is not a contract: ownership. Again, by ownership, I mean the possession of the *residual rights of control* as well as (at least some of) the *residual income rights*. As we will see, decision rights can be *partitioned*, and some rights, notably usufruct rights, can in part be contracted away.

In a classic owner-managed firm, all is straightforward. The owner possesses both the residual claim and the residual control rights, and parting with the totality of those rights is the same as selling the firm. But what about the separation of ownership and control? If a firm is "owned" by diffuse stockholders but run by salaried managers, have the owners not parted with the right of control? Maybe the managers are really the true "owners" of the firm. Henry Hansmann (1996) has argued persuasively that what matters is not de facto control but the formal (de jure) rights of control. More interestingly, he argued, it may actually be efficient to grant the rights of control to parties who may not be able to exercise them all that effectively. In the case of the managerial firm, making the managers the formal owners would only *increase* the ability of those managers to enrich themselves at the expense of their contracting parties, including the parties – the stockholders – who supplied them with capital. Even though stockholders don't have direct operating control on the ground, they can nonetheless provide some check on the behavior of managers through the market for corporate control and other mechanisms (Jensen and Meckling 1976). And firms in which the capital suppliers retain formal control might thus be more valuable and successful than firms in which the capital suppliers ceded all control rights to salaried managers.

By focusing on the formal rights of control, Hansmann is able to break the nexus that is the firm into two kinds of relationships: ownership and contract. One set of relational parties – Hansmann calls them "patrons" – holds the formal rights of control and the residual claims; all other patrons receive limited rights and duties specified by contract. The analytical exercise is then a matter of understanding when and why one set of patrons is the owner and the other patrons are contractual partners. This, in turn, is a matter of toting up and comparing, for each possible assignment of ownership, the costs of ownership and the costs of contracting. In this way, Hansmann is able to generalize the idea of "the firm." For although we most often think of – and most often find – enterprises owned by the suppliers of capital, the world is actually full of enterprises owned by other patrons, including workers, customers, or suppliers. In the end, all enterprises are really *co-ops*.

This is true even of the conventional firm, which is in the end a *capital cooperative*. Although some capital is typically supplied through contract, in the form of bonds or bank loans, it is ultimately the suppliers of capital – the shareholders – who hold the residual claim and the residual rights of control. This is because, of all the patrons, the suppliers of capital typically face the highest costs of being contractors. When I take out my wallet, hand you money, and ask you to return it eventually with a profit, I am generating a serious principal-agent problem. It is a problem so large that, most of the time, the costs it generates outweigh the obvious costs of having to monitor managers, including the costs of collective action among diffuse stockholders. "Ownership of the firm by contributors of capital … largely removes this problem by putting the contributors of capital on both sides of the transaction, in the form of equity investors (i.e., shareholders) who are both lenders to, and owners of, the firm" (Hansmann 2014, p. 3).

This is a different argument from the more common one that suppliers of capital are owners because they have the greatest wherewithal to bear the possibility of negative residual claims. Resources are certainly an issue, notably when production requires large physical-capital investments. Frank Knight (1921) long ago argued that the firm arises because one group of patrons must exercise a guaranteeing function, making sure that the contracts with the various non-owning parties are honored. But there is more involved in a guarantee than merely having resources. The owners must also persuade the contracting parties that they (the owners) will not – cannot – withdraw those resources unexpectedly (Blair 2003). As Hansmann and Reinier Kraakman (2000) have argued, creating such guarantees cannot be accomplished through contract alone; it requires the construction of specific institutions within corporate law.

One folk account of the corporation is that it arises to provide owners with limited liability, making the private assets of owners safe from the creditors of the corporation. But limiting the liability of known voluntary creditors could, in principle, be handled entirely through contract; it is merely a feature that the contracting parties can "price in" ex ante.[1] Hansmann and Kraakman (2000) argue that it is the opposite kind of limited liability that requires corporate law – and that defines the firm. By creating the firm as a "legal person," the law partitions assets into a private sphere and a corporate sphere. It does so not to protect the assets of the private owners from the creditors of the corporation but rather to protect the assets of the corporation from the creditors of the private owners. This kind of partitioning cannot be accomplished through case-by-case contracts, since the costs of identifying and bargaining with all the creditors of the capital suppliers, including unknown future ones, would be prohibitive. Asset partitioning must be established in corporate law.

The creation of an artificial entity legally separate from, even if owned by, the capital suppliers better enables those capital suppliers to guarantee

---

[1]   The same is not true for limited tort liability – liability against "involuntary creditors." Limiting that kind of liability would always require corporate law.

the contracts of the other cooperating parties.[2] For one thing, the corporation – unlike a private individual – does not have a fixed lifespan. The ability to create perpetually lived organizations is a key feature of the liberal open-access orders that have been crucial for modern economic growth (North, Wallis and Weingast 2009, p. 23).

Box 6.1 The state as a corporation

We think of political states and business firms as very different things. And in many ways, they are. But along some important dimensions, they are quite similar. Indeed, municipalities, as well as religious orders and universities, were incorporated in post-Roman Europe long before business enterprises were (Greif 2006).

Max Weber (1978, p. 54) famously defined a state as an entity that holds a monopoly on the legitimate use of physical force. And, although there are certainly exceptions – the British East India Company comes to mind – private corporations do not wield, let alone monopolize, violence. (Mercenaries and defense contractors do not themselves wield force; they sell on markets the capacity to deploy violence.) Nonetheless, states arguably have some firm-like characteristics. Riffing on Weber, Douglass North (1981, p. 23) modeled the state as a single-owner firm that is a natural monopolist in the use of force. While providing only minimally necessary public goods, the owner – the ruler – tries to maximize revenue from taxation (broadly understood), subject to the constraint that the populace not revolt.

But history also reveals a quite different model of the state – the state as a co-op (Hansmann 2014). With the revival of trade in the eleventh and twelfth centuries, the merchant class became increasingly important in cities, displacing control by bishops and nobles and organizing municipal institutions for their own benefit (Pirenne 1925). In effect, the city became a club of its middle-class residents. The residents

---

[2] The fact that the corporation is a legal person – a "legal fiction" – has led many to argue that, like a natural person, a corporation has no owners. The only thing shareholders own is their shares. But this is wrong. For the reasons Hansmann (1996) articulates, because holders of common stock collectively hold the residual rights of control, they are indeed the owners of the capital cooperative. There is no reason that the corporation cannot be at once a legal person and an ownable entity (Langlois 2019).

agreed to tax themselves in order to provide public goods, like the maintenance of city walls and the administration of justice, that they couldn't have provided individually. Think of it as a bit like a modern-day real estate condominium on a grander scale. In a condominium, owners possess their own units in fee simple, but they also must contribute a condo fee for the maintenance of public amenities and agree to be "governed" by a representative condo board. Of course, historical city-states deviated from the ideal type, and most acted as territorial governments at some times and in some respects, including going to war. In addition, free cities in history were sometimes, though by no means always, under the protection of external territorial rulers, who frequently offered "protection" in both senses of the term (Tilly 1985).

In his later work (with John Wallis and Barry Weingast), North revised the single-owner model (North, Wallis and Weingast 2009). Very often, in both history and the modern world, an extractive state is ruled not by a single owner but by a coalition, an organizational form not unlike a commercial partnership. Violence, after all, is costly. If competing would-be violence monopolists could figure out how to cooperate with each other, they could effectively share a "peace dividend." When this happens, the result is what North, Wallis, and Weingast call the *natural state*. In order to keep the rents flowing, and thus to keep the arrangement relatively stable, the dominant coalition must limit access to rights and privileges, including the right to form perpetually lived organizations.

As we see all around us in today's world, the problem with natural states is that although they benefit the ruling coalition, they limit the kind of modern economic growth that would lift the vast populations they rule out of poverty. A handful of polities, what we think of as modern liberal democracies, have managed to move beyond the natural state to become *open-access orders*. In an open-access order, rights are widely and anonymously shared. They do not depend on membership in the coalition. Aided by perpetually lived organizations, notably corporations, such societies can generate economic growth and widespread prosperity.

And when a natural state transitions to an open-access order, it transforms into something very like a business corporation. As in a capital cooperative, the state is "owned" by a large and diffuse constituency – citizen voters – who provide the funding but face high costs of exercising control. Indeed, at higher levels of government, the principal-agent problem of shareholders pales in comparison with that of voters, who in addition cannot legally sell their ownership (voting) rights and generally face far greater costs of exit. Yet, once again, it is preferable to place the rights of residual control in the hands of patrons not cheaply able to exercise those rights, since to do otherwise – to grant the control rights to manager-rulers – would be worse: it would recreate a natural state. Of course, unlike corporate shareholders, voters can never expect that their residual income claims will ever be positive (income redistribution aside). Citizens must pay taxes.

Although ownership by capital suppliers is the most common organizational form, it is by no means the only alternative. There are many situations in which ownership by a different set of patrons is a better choice. Consider the worker-owned firm. The idea that workers might own and control their own workplaces has long been a dream in Western thought, and many have lamented the paucity of worker-owned enterprises in advanced modern economies. In fact, even though they most certainly account for a far smaller fraction of output than capitalist-owned firms, worker-owned firms are not, in fact, rare. What are rare are firms owned in a meaningful sense by proletarians.[3]

Workers can be owners in the sense that they can be shareholders. Many firms sell or give shares to workers, effectively making them capital suppliers as well as workers; in a few rare cases, employees are the firm's only owners in this sense.[4] And, of course, workers can be stockholders through employee stock-ownership plans (ESOPs) or retirement accounts. Peter Drucker (1976) long ago called this pension-fund

---

[3]   In Marx, a proletarian is anyone who sells his or her labor on a market. I mean it here in the more colloquial sense of unskilled labor. Chapters 7 and 8 think harder about the meaning of "skill."

[4]   An example is the Chinese telecommunications firm Huawei, which is owned by a holding company that is in turn owned almost entirely, and only, by current and retired employees, operating through a cooperative entity that labels itself a trade union. Unlike in an American-style ESOP, in which voting rights do not pass through to employees but are typically held by a trustee board (Hansmann 1996, p. 107), Huawei employees have direct voting rights. Founder Ren Zhengfei personally owns about one percent of the holding company and possesses a veto over certain kinds of decisions. This structure evolved to evade problems created by the constraints and limitations of developing Chinese corporate law and "industrial policy" (Hawes 2021).

socialism: workers were coming increasingly to own title to the means of production. At the same time, there are also many firms out there that are genuine worker cooperatives. But the workers in those firms are typically not proletarians; they are well-compensated knowledge workers like doctors, lawyers, accountants, and consultants.[5]

Consider, with Barzel (1987), an artisan who knows how to make a nifty specialized gizmo but knows little about business – little about marketing, buying materials, getting credit, or setting up a factory. She could hire a knowledge worker with an MBA to supply those skills at a fixed wage. But that would be a hazardous arrangement, since the artisan wouldn't easily be able to tell whether the MBA is doing a good job or is shirking. Alternatively, they could form a firm. But who should own it? That depends on the total costs of the alternatives, including monitoring and moral-hazard costs. If both contribute equally to the value of the firm, the owner should be whichever one is more difficult to monitor (all other things being equal). If the MBA's tasks are varied and harder to quantify – unlike, perhaps, the output of the artisan, which can easily be inspected and counted – then the MBA should possess the residual rights. Those residual rights, as Barzel puts it, are the entrepreneur's reward for self-policing. Of course, if she is paid a wage, the artisan will then shirk, but that may be better than the alternatives, especially since the MBA could potentially share some of the usufruct with the artisan, including through the kinds of share contracts common in agriculture.

Knowledge workers are frequently organized as worker co-ops, especially when, as is typically the case in professional services, there is little non-human capital involved. For example, physicians often own their own practices, taking advantage of physical capital like a hospital that is owned by others (sometimes a non-profit organization), which they share with other physicians as a quasi-public good. As the theory predicts, physicians with specialties that are both valuable and hard to monitor (like brain surgery) are likely to own their own practices, whereas physicians with more easily monitored specialties (like pathology or radiology) are hired in many cases as employees, either of hospitals or of capital-owned practices.[6] Again, it is total costs that matter, not just monitoring

---

5   Or private detectives, as Frank Knight (1921, p. 255) adds.

6   According to the American Medical Association, the fraction of physicians who work in practices that are wholly owned by physicians has been declining and has now dropped below 50 percent (Kane 2021).

costs. Physicians pursuing life-and-death specialties (brain surgery) may be more valuable than less-critical specialties (pathology) even if they are not harder to monitor. As Barzel and Allen (2023, p. 133) put it, "the greater the inclination of a productive factor to affect the mean outcome, the greater the claim on the residual that that input owner will assume."

But a word of caution is in order. Possession of the residual claims creates an incentive for the owners, in this case, the highly valuable knowledge workers, to work hard, innovate, and use local knowledge that other patrons don't have access to. This is far more than just a matter of being unable to "measure" worker output. In employee-owned law firms, for example, workers keep detailed accounts of how their time – their billable hours – is allocated to tasks. Indeed, Hansmann (1996, p. 96) argues that an ability to calculate relatively objective marginal products can often be crucial to making a worker-owned cooperative successful. When the owners have highly divergent interests and incentives, management becomes difficult, and conflict becomes a threat. Thus, worker-owned firms often use simple or easily verified sharing rules to avoid conflict.

It is, of course, one of the great virtues of the capital co-op that its owners have highly homogeneous goals, and this homogeneity of interest is one of the reasons that ownership by capital is the default form of organization.[7] There is certainly a large literature extolling the virtues of granting

---

Great care must be exercised in analyzing the organizational structure of healthcare, of course, since in the U.S. (as elsewhere) that industry is heavily regulated, and Medicare and Medicaid, with their complex rules for reimbursement, loom large. With technological change, the minimum efficient scale for many surgeries and other procedures has been declining, leading to the rise of specialized ambulatory care centers. In the early twenty-first century, physician ownership of these facilities grew rapidly, despite federal and state regulations limiting such ownership (Baum 2010). In 2010, the Patient Protection and Affordable Care Act made physician ownership of such facilities illegal. Private equity has stepped into the breach and is now increasingly buying up medical practices.

[7]   Milton Friedman famously argued that the only responsibility of corporations – he actually talked about the employees of corporations – is to fulfill the wishes of the owners of the corporation, whatever those wishes might be. He did not say that the only goal of the corporation should be to make a profit (even though the writer of the headline in the *New York Times Magazine* did say that). Generally, but not always, Friedman thought, the owners would want to make as much money as possible,

workers on the shop floor at least some decision-making authority and of learning from them. But that is a far cry from giving easy-to-monitor workers veto power and full "democratic" control over the workplace. "Employee ownership offers much stronger efficiencies than it is generally credited with, and would be far more widespread if it were not critically handicapped by the very thing that is often considered its greatest virtue, namely, the opportunity it affords for active worker participation in governance" (Hansmann 1996, p. 5).

Ownership by workers is by no means the only alternative to ownership by capital. Especially in the agricultural sector, *seller cooperatives* – co-ops owned by farmers selling agricultural commodities – are extremely common. Most people do not realize that many businesses they assume are ordinary capitalist firms are, in fact, co-ops. It comes as a surprise that brands like Ocean Spray, Land O'Lakes, Cabot, Sunkist, and Diamond are owned by the farmers who supply the agricultural inputs.

To a perhaps astonishing degree, farming – the actual tilling of the soil and growing of crops – is still undertaken in the modern-day U.S. by family firms, which sometimes own and sometimes lease the land (Allen and Lueck 2004). This is despite technological change and the increased capital intensity of farming. The wide variety of tasks required in farming, along with the vagaries of nature, demand a system of incentives that rewards tillers of the soil with residual claims and accords them residual control. But some stages of agricultural production are predictable enough that they can, in fact, be accomplished with economies of scale. (Think back to stage D in Figure 1.3.) In agriculture, this typically means the stages of processing and marketing, which involve relatively predictable tasks and take place off the land.

If one processing plant can serve many, many farmers, that plant will be a bottleneck stage, in effect a local monopsony. The result would be not only a transfer of rents away from the farmers but also an inefficiency, since a monopsonist will want to buy too low an amount of crop and offer too low a price for it. This creates an incentive for the farmers themselves to band together to own the processing stage. Such an arrangement will be efficient when the costs of farmer ownership are less than the

---

and managers should accommodate, while adhering to the "basic rules of the society, both those embodied in law and those embodied in ethical custom" (Friedman 1970, p. 33).

efficiency gains from eliminating the monopsony (all other things equal). Once again, a divergence of interests among the owners can increase the costs of ownership. This is why agricultural co-ops tend to restrict themselves to one or a few similar crops in which the farmers have relatively homogeneous interests and share a common stock of knowledge.

Notice that in this arrangement, farmers are also the suppliers of capital, even if some capital can be rented from banks and bondholders. Co-ops of this sort can be innovative – as Ocean Spray notably has been – so long as the innovation doesn't disrupt the commonality of interests. But the difficulty of raising new capital places limitations on the co-op form, especially when capital has to be raised in large amounts at short notice. In 2004, Ocean Spray farmers narrowly voted against selling the company to PepsiCo (Cohen 2023), with which the co-op has had an on-and-off distribution and bottling partnership.

Similarly, *customer cooperatives* might form to circumvent a potential monopoly (rather than monopsony) stage of production. In 1846, what became the Associated Press formed as a co-op of local newspapers, initially in New York City. The problem was the telegraph, which created a bottleneck on news emerging from the war in Mexico (John 2010, p. 10). It soon became clear that gathering national and international news was an activity with economies of scale, and expanding the co-op form made sense. Customer co-ops are probably more familiar in retailing, even if few people are aware that brands like Ace Hardware, True Value Hardware, and IGA (Independent Grocers Association) stores are actually co-ops: it is the local stores that own the brand name and some of the purchasing and logistics stages of production. Although retail-goods cooperatives owned by final consumers do exist – to a greater extent in the U.K. than in the U.S. – these are relatively rare, as the transaction costs of identifying customers are high, and in any case, the final retail stage is typically highly competitive.[8] But co-ops owned by final con-

---

[8]   The retail stage was less competitive and more localized in an earlier world of high transportation and transaction costs. Retail co-ops persisted for a long time in one area – the university bookstore – which often held something of a natural monopoly at the campus level on textbook sales and served buyers who were easy to identify and whose custom was predictable. With the rise of internet book sales, however, these have largely now disappeared, including at my own university, which has partnered with Barnes & Noble, a capital-owned chain increasingly specialized in running college bookstores.

sumers are common in financial services like mutual funds and mutual insurance companies (that's what the "mutual" part means).

In the case of customer cooperatives like hardware and grocery stores, the bottlenecks in the chain of production are in purchasing and warehouse logistics, which benefit from economies of scale. In addition, and perhaps more importantly, centralized branding and advertising are public goods in which all the members of the co-op can share. (This is true in the case of seller cooperatives like Ocean Spray as well, of course.) So, as in the case of seller co-ops, it may make sense for a highly decentralized stage of production to own the more centralized stages. Such an arrangement preserves high-powered incentives at the decentralized stage without generating great costs to the more centralized stages (at least, once again, if there is enough homogeneity of interests among the decentralized owners that ownership costs do not become too high).

There is one significant difference between farmers and retail stores, however. Because of the task structure of working the land, the husbandry stages of production in agriculture remain stubbornly decentralized in ownership. But in retailing, a growing extent of the market can easily remove any monopoly in stages like purchasing, logistics, and warehousing, thereby eliminating the driving logic of the cooperative form and opening the way for capital ownership of the whole chain of production. Indeed, big-box stores like Home Depot, Lowe's, and Walmart have come to dominate retail sectors that had once been the province of co-ops, pushing the likes of Ace, True Value, and IGA into small niche markets. Big-city dailies and broadcast networks long ago integrated into their own national and international newsgathering, though AP still exists as a co-op serving a multitude of smaller outlets.

Eliminating local ownership always has its costs, since hired managers might shirk more than owner-managers. The solution is often to create an alternative form of organization that partitions tasks and asset ownership. One such form is *franchising*. Under a franchise arrangement, capital owns the parts of the process best suited to capital ownership, while decentralized patrons retain residual claims. Blair and Lafontaine (2006, p. 55) observe that "the main advantage of franchising over vertically integrated operations arises from its unique combination of (1) the chain's comparative advantages in creating brand recognition and capturing economies of scale in production, product development, and advertising with (2) the independent entrepreneur's drive and knowledge of the local market. In other words, in the ideal franchise relationship, each party is allowed to specialize in what it does best." Like co-ops, franchises – perhaps best known in the fast-food sector – are ubiquitous.

A franchise arrangement bears a strong resemblance to a buyer's co-op. In a franchise, however, rather than owning the more centralized stages of production, the decentralized buyers hire the services of those stages on contract, retaining the residual claims only to their own operations. For services like purchasing and logistics, contracting costs may well be low. But one crucial factor looms large. In a buyer's co-op, the decentralized buying stage owns the collective brand-name capital; in a franchise, the decentralized stage rents the services of the brand-name capital on contract. Brand-name capital is a public good. So, although they have the incentive to work hard and use their local knowledge effectively, individual franchisees also have an incentive to free ride – by skimping on maintenance or the quality of inputs, for example – at the expense of the brand name. Free riding is a danger even when the decentralized buyers themselves own the brand, of course, though they may be in a better position than an outside owner to police one another. But brand-name free riding looms large in franchising. Trademark owners often expend resources on monitoring, and franchise contracts are typically larded with restrictions to protect the brand name.

One way to mitigate free riding would be for the franchisor to require the franchisees to buy all their inputs directly from the trademark owner. In the 1950s and 1960s, Chicken Delight was a pioneer in the home delivery of fast food, a service with which we are now so familiar. Because of quality-control problems, the chain demanded that its franchisees buy crucial inputs only from the chain itself. Precisely because they wanted to free ride by using cheaper inputs, some of the franchisees sued Chicken Delight under the Sherman Antitrust Act. An appeals court upheld the guilty verdict of the district court, invalidating the franchise contracts.[9] (Later courts would reverse this precedent, and input tying for quality control is now widely used.)

More generally, it has been common throughout history for a decentralized user base to rent the services of large capital assets through contract.

---

[9]   *Siegel v. Chicken Delight, Inc.*, 311 F. Supp. 847 (N.D. Cal. 1970). The court saw the arrangement as an illegal tying agreement, a topic to which we will turn presently. Chicken Delight quickly went out of business, leaving the franchisees (including the plaintiffs) worse off.

In the Lancashire cotton textile industry of the Industrial Revolution, the multitudes of small spinners and weavers seldom owned their own factories but would typically "lease room and turning" – rent space and power – from independent mill owners (Farnie 1979, p. 271). Because textile machinery was relatively inexpensive in the early years, firms bought rather than leased their machines, though the machinery-makers often loaned them the money and always supplied know-how and maintenance services. In the U.S. in the twentieth century, United Shoe Machinery leased rather than sold its panoply of shoe-making machines to a large base of small shoemakers, also supplying design and maintenance services. IBM leased rather than sold its mainframes for similar reasons. As in franchising, users may not always have good incentives to maintain rented capital, and they may be able to free ride on public goods like setup and design services. As a result, lease contracts are often filled with restrictions to prevent free riding. These practices too drew forth antitrust suits. The Justice Department successfully sued both United Shoe and IBM.[10]

Indeed, a central theme in American antitrust law has been an episodic antagonism to complex contracting.[11] Although much of this policy was certainly driven by public-choice factors, it also has roots in the pervasive bare-bones neoclassical model of the firm, which had (and has) no mechanism for understanding why complex contracting might be efficient in a world of transaction costs. As Coase put it, "if an economist finds something — a business practice of one sort or other — that he does not understand, he looks for a monopoly explanation. And as in this field we are very ignorant, the number of ununderstandable practices tends to be rather large, and the reliance on a monopoly explanation, frequent" (Coase 1972, p. 67). Williamson would brand this attitude "the inhospitality tradition" (Williamson 1983a, p. 292). In the 1960s, he complained, economists were working with "a black box theory of the firm and a plain vanilla theory of markets" (Williamson 2009, p. 12).

---

[10] For a dissection of the *United Shoe* case, see Masten and Snyder (1993), and for the *IBM* case, see Fisher, McKie, and Mancke (1983).

[11] For a more careful analysis of the history of antitrust from an organizational perspective, see Langlois (2023). Note that since vertical integration is an institutional substitute for (sporadically criminalized) complex contracting, much of antitrust policy has arguably reinforced the vertically integrated firm more than it has fostered market competition.

No form of complex contracting has been more central to debates about antitrust than *tying arrangements* like the one used by Chicken Delight. In the end, what a consumer is buying is always a service, even if the consumer buys a product or products in order to generate the service. The provision of a valuable service typically involves a system of complementary parts.[12] If the services of some of those components are hard to measure, and especially if they display economies of scale (and are effectively public goods), purveyors can seize efficiencies by tying the purchase of a hard-to-measure component to the purchase of one that is easier to measure.

In the days of mechanical information processing, IBM would assemble systems of complementary components to fit the needs of users (Usselman 1993), including devices employing the punched cards invented by Herman Hollerith in the nineteenth century. It was IBM's policy to demand that buyers of mechanical equipment using punched cards buy their cards only from IBM itself. There were two reasons for this. Like Chicken Delight, IBM was concerned about quality control. Users might buy cheap cards that would jam the equipment, harming IBM's brand-name capital. In addition, information-processing systems were large, lumpy purchases, so the purchase conveyed little information to IBM about the intensity of the user's demand. By tying the cards to the machines, IBM could measure user demand more finely, thus enabling the firm to price discriminate. (Although price discrimination transfers rents away from some buyers – and is thus hated by such buyers – it is not generally inefficient, as it allows more Pareto-improving trades to take place.)

Much of the technology IBM leased was protected by patents. In the view of the courts, and indeed of most people, the problem with tying arrangements is that they allow a patent holder to "leverage" its patent monopoly into the tied good.[13] In effect, they believed, tying punched cards to leased data-processing equipment could create a second monopoly in punched cards.[14] By the late 1950s, however, some scholars had begun to question

---

[12]   Chapter 9 explores such systems in greater detail.

[13]   As the Supreme Court would declare in 1953, the "essence of illegality in tying agreements is the wielding of monopolistic leverage." *Times-Picayune Pub. Co. v. United States*, 345 U.S. 594 (1953).

[14]   A few years earlier, the great Louis D. Brandeis argued in another case that the holder of a patent on an icebox could use tying to leverage its market power into dry ice: "the owner of a patent for a product might

this logic (Bowman 1957; Director and Levi 1956). What the consumer is actually buying are data-processing services, which require both machinery and cards. The seller can allocate the price of data-processing services between the two necessary components (equipment and cards); but it will not benefit from raising the total price of services above the optimal price that its (patent-induced) market power dictates. In a simple tying case like this one, there is only one "lump" of monopoly, and tying cannot make it bigger. This logic applies widely, including to one of today's controversial issues, the phenomenon of an Internet platform like Amazon or Google "self-preferencing" its own products.[15]

In the end, contracts are always about restriction. In a deep sense, it is precisely the ability to write contracts of exclusion that makes a competitive market function well. Consider the practice of *resale price maintenance*. Here, a manufacturer or distributor demands that retailers not compete on price but set a price determined by the manufacturer or distributor.[16] On the surface, this too looks anticompetitive, since it prevents retailers from competing on price. In fact, however, it is – once again – a mechanism for reducing a free-riding problem. Especially for products that are new or complex, manufacturers may want to eliminate reseller price competition in order to force competition to take place along various non-price margins, especially sales effort and pre- or post-sales

---

conceivably monopolize the commerce in a large part of unpatented materials used in its manufacture. The owner of a patent for a machine might thereby secure a partial monopoly on the unpatented supplies consumed in its operation" (*Carbice Corp. v. Patents Development Corp.*, 283 U.S. 31 (1931).) Indeed, Brandeis feared, the patent holder might even leverage its monopoly into ice cream. In reality, the patent almost certainly didn't even give Carbice a monopoly over iceboxes (Hovenkamp 2005, p. 33), which were in any case a declining industry: by 1931 firms like GE, Frigidaire (owned by GM), and Kelvinator were already selling millions of mechanical refrigerators a year.

[15]   If another firm produces a component that is *superior* to the system-seller's own version, then the seller has an incentive to tie (or at least to "preference") *someone else's* product in order to make the system as a whole more attractive to consumers. How the rents of such an arrangement are distributed would fall to a Coasean bargain.

[16]   Private resale price maintenance contracts are entirely different from state-imposed resale price maintenance, sometimes called "fair trade" laws. Fair trade is all about legally protecting small competitors by preventing larger and more efficient firms from competing on price.

service.[17] If some resellers are allowed to discount, customers can free ride on the services of the non-discounters and then buy from the discounters, which will create an incentive for no one to provide the services and sales effort (Telser 1960). A similar logic lies behind exclusive dealing arrangements and territorial restrictions (Klein and Murphy 1988; Williamson 1985, pp. 183–189).

In the end, then, there is a vast range of economic activity lying between the extremes of market and firm or, to use Williamson's language, of market and hierarchy. In his early work, Williamson not only adhered to a clear distinction between markets and hierarchies but also held that intermediate arrangements were unstable. In later work, however, he became "persuaded that transactions in the middle range are much more common" (Williamson 1985, p. 83). He even gave a name to these intermediate organizational structures: they are *hybrids* (Williamson 1991). In essence, hybrid forms represent a compromise between the high-powered incentives of markets at one extreme and the coordination benefits of hierarchy at the other. The idea of hybrid forms took off in the literature, driven by the late-twentieth-century fragmentation of once vertically integrated firms into networks of subcontracting, joint ventures, and other complex relationships.[18] Soon everything became a "hybrid," and the concept began to degenerate into the same kind of vagueness as the nexus-of-contracts view of the firm (Hodgson 2002).

Yet, if we retain the conceptually – and legally – distinct categories of ownership and contract, this intermediate category can remain both sharp and useful. Claude Ménard (2021, p. 302) defines hybrids as "arrangements in which two or more partners pool strategic decision rights as well as some property rights, passing these rights across fixed boundaries of organizations that remain legally distinct and keep autonomous control over key assets." This arguably describes the complex contracting structures we have just seen.

---

[17]   Although he completely fanned on tying, Brandeis (1913) early on penned what is in many ways a Coasean analysis of resale price maintenance, placing him far ahead of contemporary economists (Breit 1991). Brandeis understood that outlawing the practice would create an incentive for vertical integration and would harm the small businesses he championed.

[18]   What I have called the Vanishing Hand (Langlois 2003).

In all the organizational forms we have looked at so far, the key issue has been the assignment of ownership – of the residual rights of control and the residual income. But there is a large class of organizations in which *no one* formally possesses ownership: non-profits. Non-profits are more accurately called *not-for-profit* entities, since what distinguishes them is not whether they make a profit but rather that they are legally prohibited from *distributing* any profit (or, for that matter, any loss) to patrons.[19] Sometimes transaction-cost, incentive, and knowledge problems are so severe that the best solution is for *no* class of patrons to own the enterprise.

Especially in the service sector, notably healthcare, non-profit firms like hospitals and nursing homes coexist with for-profit firms; the two forms often look a lot alike.[20] This suggests that under some circumstances, alternate solutions to the ownership problem can get similar results, which means in turn that path dependency may be important (Hansmann 1988, pp. 236–237). (Chapter 9 will examine this concept in greater detail.) But in some spheres of activity, non-profits dominate.

We saw that the problem faced by investors – taking out your wallet and entrusting others with the money – creates powerful principal-agent problems. Those problems are magnified when the owner of the wallet expects a negative return by design – is intentionally giving the money away – and there are no good measures of whether the organization is using the money well. If you donate to an organization that promises to educate the poor or fight climate change, you know you won't get your money back, and you typically have no way of determining whether your wishes are really being fulfilled. If the organization to which you donate operates under a non-distribution constraint, all of those problems are not solved, but at least you know that your donation cannot be legitimately diverted into the pockets of any but the intended beneficiaries. Cynical economists suggest that at least one component of the motive for donating to charity arises from the public cachet or private warm glow of the gift, and donating to a for-profit entity would diminish the

---

19   In a long-ago conversation with someone who worked at a famous non-profit research institute, I asked what happened when the institute, which had numerous government and private contracts, made a profit. "We put a new wing on the building," I was told.

20   Non-profits in manufacturing are virtually non-existent – again because manufacturing requires significant capital, and the output of manufacturing workers is typically easy to monitor.

cachet and reduce the warm glow, meaning fewer donations. In the case of purely donative activities, then, the benefits of having no owner can outweigh the loss of the incentives for efficiency that ownership brings.

To put it another way, a non-profit (rather than a co-op) may arise when buyers or sellers are more worried about the ability of a production stage to skimp on quality than they are about its ability to exercise power over price (Hansmann 1996, p. 243). Co-ops and non-profits are closely related: indeed, many kinds of clubs are organized as not-for-profit firms rather than as co-ops. As we saw, the success of a co-op depends on the costs of exercising ownership, and that, in turn, depends significantly on the stability of ownership and the costs of identifying potential owners in the first place. A non-profit may be the better alternative when club membership is fluid and changeable.

Box 6.2   The American research university

The university is a particularly complex example of non-profit governance. As seen from Europe and other places around the world, the American version of the research university looks particularly weird: many of the best ones are not owned by the state, and they bundle education not only with large-scale scientific research but also – and far more mysteriously – with big-time semi-professional athletics. (In fact, the private university sector is growing around the world, and universities in many countries are actually owned by the family foundations of large business groups (Altbach, Choi, Allen and de Wit 2019).)

In Europe after the fall of Rome, what higher learning there was took place in a monastic setting; it was effectively professional training for monks and priests. With the economic and intellectual renaissance of the twelfth century, however, demand increased for education outside the monastery, including tutoring in more secular subjects like philosophy – with the rediscovery of ancient classical texts – and in subjects of practical use like law and medicine. In order to generate and share public goods, especially brand-name capital, both students and teachers formed co-ops. "The university was originally a scholastic guild whether of masters or students," wrote the nineteenth-century philosopher Hastings Rashdall (1895, p. 15) in his classic study of the medieval university. "Such guilds sprang into existence, like other guilds, without any express authorization of king, pope, prince, or prelate. They were spontaneous products of that instinct of association which swept like a great wave over the towns of Europe in the course of the eleventh and twelfth centuries." The preeminent University of Paris began as a teacher co-op, while the equally preeminent University of Bologna began as a student co-op.

Because students and faculty come and go, a literal co-op was not a long-term solution, and universities quickly incorporated as what were essentially non-profits, becoming perpetually lived organizations. Yet they remained clubs, and the faculty remained owners in fundamental respects, exercising residual control through democratic processes much like voters in a polity. Using their powers of exclusion, universities then as now sought out the best students and faculty in order to increase the organization's reputational capital and earn both pecuniary and non-pecuniary rents for its members. In modern lingo, the consumers of education were also *co-producers* of that education: "What is particularly interesting about these organizations is the unusual source of their market power vis-à-vis their consumers, which often derives from the personal characteristics of the consumers themselves" (Hansmann 1996, p. 194).

In the U.S. in the nineteenth century, higher education was dominated by denominational liberal arts colleges dedicated mostly to producing clergymen. As the demand for more rigorous and extensive professional training increased toward the end of the century, a new institution emerged – the research university – highly influenced by German models (Veysey 1965). Some private colleges (like Harvard, Yale, and Princeton) and some state-owned universities (like Michigan and Wisconsin) adapted slowly to the new model, but the most prominent universities were newly created ones (like Chicago, Clark, Cornell, Johns Hopkins, and Stanford) bankrolled by industrialists. Whereas liberal arts colleges had been relatively hierarchical in structure, the better to prosecute what was often a coherent religious mission, the new American university was closer to the medieval model of a club. The empirical evidence is that today non-sectarian private universities are organized in a more decentralized, "democratic" fashion than state universities or Catholic-affiliated ones, which require more hierarchical control to respond coherently to an outside constituency (Masten 2006).

It is easy to see why universities would bundle research and teaching. Even though individual faculty members most certainly feel teaching and research as substitute claims on their time, from the perspective of the university, there are significant economies of scope between the two endeavors. But why bundle Division I sports with teaching and research?

Because their outputs are so hard to measure, the most crucial knowledge workers of the university – the faculty – enjoy considerable discretion. But they are not the only constituency in the club. Students are crucial, both because they help to produce the very reputational capital they enjoy and because they are an important source of donations. Unlike theater patrons, who engage in voluntary price discrimination (donation) at the same time they are buying tickets, students do not typically become donors until long after they have consumed the services for which they paid tuition. This means that the university must continue to engage the students as members of the club even after they have graduated – and sports are a good way to do that. In effect, sports create a second form of reputational capital that, through donations, is complementary to the university's academic reputational capital. Clark Kerr, the president of the University of California system in the 1960s, famously joked that a university has three purposes: "to provide sex for the students, sports for the alumni, and parking for the faculty."

Many non-profits arise to provide public goods (or assets with economies of scale) to a decentralized base, serving much the same function as a co-op. We have already seen the example of hospitals, which are often (though by no means always) non-profits, supplying plant, equipment, and other services for a decentralized network of doctors and other medical professionals. As with co-ops, many non-profits of this kind were originally brought into existence by that decentralized professional base itself, precisely to provide those capital goods. Hospitals in the U.S. were typically founded by physicians.[21] In the arts, many museums, theaters, and opera halls were formed as clubs of (a constantly changing mix of) arts patrons. Interestingly, patrons of the arts contribute not only by buying the services of the non-profit through tickets but also by making donations. This is a kind of voluntary price discrimination that helps to

---

[21]   Because of ethnic discrimination, Catholic and Jewish doctors in the early twentieth century seldom had privileges at the mainline Protestant hospitals, so they formed their own hospital-clubs (Lazarus 1991). Hartford, Connecticut, had three hospitals: Hartford Hospital (Protestant), St. Francis (Catholic), and Mt. Sinai (Jewish).

cover fixed costs (Hansmann 1996, p. 232). Indeed, since big donors are almost always numerous or important on non-profit boards, meaning that donors exercise some degree of control over the organization, we might even think of a donative non-profit as a kind of donors' co-op.

Suggested readings

Yoram Barzel, "The Entrepreneur's Reward for Self-Policing," *Economic Inquiry* **25**(1): 103–116, 1987.

Roger D. Blair and Francine Lafontaine, "Understanding the Economics of Franchising and the Laws That Regulate It," *Franchise Law Journal* **26**(2): 55–66, 2006.

Henry Hansmann, *The Ownership of Enterprise*. Cambridge: Belknap Press, 1996.

Henry Hansmann and Reinier Kraakman, "Organization Law as Asset Partitioning," *European Economic Review* **44**(4–6): 807–817, 2000.

Benjamin Klein and Kevin M. Murphy, "Vertical Restraints as Contract Enforcement Mechanisms," *The Journal of Law and Economics* **31**(2): 265–297, 1988.

7 Capabilities, evolution, and dynamic transaction costs

We saw in Chapter 2 that the foundational insight of the economics of organization was Coase's realization that production costs alone could not explain organization. As modeled in the formal price theory then developing, production costs could not tell us why some transactions are governed through markets and others are managed within firms. Coase's solution was to create what was, in essence, a whole new category of costs – transaction costs – that did not replace neoclassical production costs but could sit on top of them to help explain the organizational structures we observe in the world.

It is hard not to see this dichotomy as a strange one. In the formal neo-classical theory that reigned for most of the twentieth century, and remains influential today, firms are understood as production functions that, much like sausage grinders, take inputs such as capital and labor and turn them into outputs in some opaque way. In order to make the construct of perfect competition work, the theory has to assume that all firms have perfect information, meaning (among other things) that everyone has exactly the same knowledge about how to produce output. All knowledge is explicit and independent of context. As Joan Robinson (1956, p. 139) famously put it, everything a firm needs to know is in the blueprints, and everyone has the same set of blueprints. This seems a wildly different epistemic environment from the one inhabited by trans-action-cost economics, where knowledge is asymmetric, uncertainty is rife, and contracts are always incomplete.

In reality, of course, producing and transacting are not fundamentally different things. Production involves a set of transactions, and transact-ing is a kind of production. Whatever theory of knowledge we employ in one realm should be consistent with the one we employ in the other. More than arguably, our theory of knowledge – in both realms – should correspond more accurately to the epistemic world that actual humans live in.

If we change how we think about knowledge in production, there are immediate implications. As Richard Nelson (1991) has long argued, firms are no longer identical. They differ in what they know and thus in how – and how well – they produce output. Indeed, the empirical evidence is that even in industries producing a homogeneous product, where one might expect something like the assumptions of perfect competition to prevail, productivity among firms differs widely: a firm in the 90th percentile is about twice as productive as one in the 10th percentile (Syverson 2011, p. 326). Needless to say, firms differ not only within an industry but – far more dramatically – across industries.

Coase himself came to worry that his own early contribution had led economists to concentrate too much on the employment relation and other contracts with factors of production. Because of this, he wrote, "economists have tended to neglect the main activity of a firm, running a business" (Coase 1988b, p. 38). As he put it elsewhere in a different context, a theory of organization should be able to explain "why General Motors was not a dominant factor in the coal industry, and why A&P did not manufacture airplanes" (Coase 1972, p. 67). This is the problem of scale and scope: how many activities does a single organization engage in? And at what scale?

Coase's 1937 paper was most notable for its account of the limits of markets: why isn't all economic activity carried out through market transactions? But he also had to address the complementary issue: "Why is not all production carried on by one big firm?"[1] (Coase 1937, p. 394). His answer was really little more than a sketch. Since management is a fixed factor of production, there must eventually come a point at which diminishing returns set in. As more and more transactions are internalized, the manager becomes overwhelmed and starts to make bad decisions: "the entrepreneur fails to place the factors of production in the uses where their value is greatest, that is, fails to make the best use of the factors of production." All well and good if we think in terms of an owner-managed

---

[1]   This problem did not trouble V. I. Lenin, who held that in the unfolding of the Marxian prediction, "the whole of society will have become one office and one factory" (Lenin 1992 [1917]).

firm, and if we don't think too hard about possible mechanisms of decentralization within the firm.

In another of the most significant papers in the history of economics, F. A. Hayek (1945) put forward a far more sophisticated account of the limits of central direction. Writing in the context of the so-called socialist calculation debate (Lavoie 1985), Hayek argued that the nature of knowledge itself sets the limits of decision-making. Far from being explicit or "scientific" knowledge easily conveyed in blueprints, the important knowledge on which both production and transaction depend is inherently local, sticky, and often tacit in the sense of Michael Polanyi (1958). Especially in a world of change, economic decision-making relies crucially on "the knowledge of the particular circumstances of time and place" (Hayek 1945, p. 522).

One immediate implication is that if knowledge is not a public good, it must be acquired locally in a process of learning. As George Richardson (1972) argued, "we cannot hope to construct an adequate theory of industrial organization and in particular to answer our question about the division of labour between firm and market, unless the elements of organisation, knowledge, experience and skills are brought back to the foreground of our vision" (Richardson 1972, p. 888). For Richardson, production requires *capabilities*: the "knowledge, experience, and skills" of the firm. It follows that as a firm acquires capabilities in a historical process over time, it will typically come to possess capabilities different from those of other firms.

To generate a capabilities account of economic organization, we need to recognize that capabilities can be either *similar* or *complementary*. (They can also be completely unrelated, of course.) Capabilities are similar when the knowledge, experience, and skills useful in activity A can be cheaply adapted to activity B. Understood in this way, "similarity" is about the process, not the product. Similar capabilities can generate very different products or services. For example, in the nineteenth century, meatpackers like Armour and Swift developed a complex set of capabilities for delivering refrigerated dressed beef to eastern cities. They soon found that they could adapt those same distribution capabilities to other kinds of dressed meat like pork and lamb; then to canned meats; then to canned seafood; and then eventually to butter, eggs, poultry, and fruit (Chandler 1977, pp. 398–399). Beef and fruit are not similar products, but the capabilities needed to distribute them were quite similar.

Both Alfred Chandler (1977) and Edith Penrose (1959) developed theories of the growth of the firm based on this idea of related capabilities. When a firm invests in the creation of capabilities – Penrose called them *resources* – it is often incurring a fixed cost. If the firm has excess capacity in these capabilities, it makes sense to go out and find new similar activities to engage in (as the meatpackers did) to spread the fixed costs over more units. But because each new activity is slightly different from previous experience, the firm finds itself having to invest in even more capabilities, albeit closely related ones. And these new capabilities may also have excess capacity. So the firm looks again for new activities to engage in. And so on. Penrose's work inspired in the management literature what came to be called the resource-based view of the firm (Wernerfelt 1984). In the end, however, the Chandler-Penrose account is really a theory of related diversification, not a full theory of the firm. Although it possesses a far better theory of knowledge in production than does the production-function approach, it doesn't seriously consider the costs of, and the possibilities for, transacting in markets (including through complex contracts) as an alternative to internal diversification (Loasby 2002, p. 52).

As we saw in Chapter 1, under the division of labor, stages of production become complementary to one another. But activities that are complementary to one another need not, and most often probably are not, similar in the sense that they require similar capabilities. The woodworking skills needed to make gun stocks are complementary to the metal-working skills needed to rifle the barrels; but those skills are not similar. "Where activities were both similar and complementary," Richardson wrote, "they could be co-ordinated by direction within an individual business. Generally, however, this would not be the case and the activities to be co-ordinated, being dissimilar, would be the responsibility of different firms. Co-ordination would then have to be brought about either through co-operation, firms agreeing to match their plans ex ante, or through the processes of adjustment set in train by the market mechanism" (Richardson 1972, p. 895). As Brian Loasby (1991, p. 81) rightly observed, this approach has the effect of standing on its head the principal presumption of transaction-cost theorists: that the world of contracting is full of "market failures" and that vertical integration is best understood as a low-cost solution to the inadequacies of the market. In fact, the difficulties of managing dissimilar activities within a single organization may outweigh contractual hazards on the whole and militate in favor of widespread disintegration.

In a fundamental sense, the question we are left with is the one we started with. Why are capabilities sometimes organized within firms, sometimes decentralized into markets, and sometimes coordinated by a myriad of overlapping contractual and ownership arrangements like joint ventures, franchises, and networks? Earlier chapters have been concerned with the question of who should get the decision rights, treating that problem as mainly (though not exclusively) one of incentives. When we take the potentially sticky, tacit, and local character of knowledge more fully into account, the problem space expands. Now we also have to consider more explicitly whether the people with the decision rights have the knowledge they need to act effectively. Echoing Hayek, Michael Jensen and William Meckling pointed out that there are basically two ways to ensure such a "collocation" of knowledge and decision-making. "One is by moving the knowledge to those with the decision rights; the other is by moving the decision rights to those with the knowledge" (Jensen and Meckling 1992, pp. 251–253).

In order to see the implications of this formulation more clearly, we first need to step back and ask some deeper methodological questions. We noted early on that the principal tool of the economics of organization, or more broadly of the New Institutional Economics, is *comparative-institutional analysis*. This approach involves placing side by side two (or more) alternative institutional structures – archetypically a market on one side and a firm or hierarchy on the other – and making arguments about which would minimize the sum of production and transaction costs under given conditions. This is an extremely powerful analytical tool. Yet it carries with it a hidden assumption – that the more efficient alternative will always be the one we observe. Indeed, economists usually work backwards: they observe an existing institutional structure and then make arguments about why it must be the alternative that minimizes the sum of production and transaction costs.[2] But exactly who or what is doing the minimizing?[3]

Mostly implicitly, but sometimes explicitly, economists have nodded at a Darwinian explanation. The organizational form we observe must

---

[2]   You've probably heard the old joke: an economist is someone who sees something working in practice and wants to know whether it would work in theory.

[3]   For a more careful and nuanced discussion of the issues in the next few paragraphs, see Langlois (1986).

minimize the sum of production and transaction costs (or, more generally, it must be "efficient") because if it didn't, it would have been replaced by some superior organizational form. There is a selection mechanism operating behind the scenes.

In the middle of the twentieth century, a controversy erupted over whether firms even maximize profits. An economist called Richard Lester sent questionnaires to American firms asking them if they behaved the way the basic model predicted, that is, whether they set price equal to marginal cost. Almost all the respondents said no; many had no idea what marginal cost meant. "We set price by simply adding a markup to what we pay for our inputs," Lester was told.[4] Not surprisingly, this ignited a heated response from mainstream economists, in what came to be called the marginalist controversy. Among those who entered the fray was Armen Alchian (1950). Suppose, said Alchian, that thousands of motorists set out from Chicago on a variety of different routes. Suppose also that there are gas stations on only one of the routes. We can safely predict that only motorists who happened to pick the route with gas stations will get very far. But we can be assured in our prediction not because we assumed any of the motorists consciously selected the best route; rather, the lucky motorists were themselves selected by the impersonal forces of the environment. What looks like fully informed rational choice is really Darwinian selection.

There were two responses to Alchian's idea (and to related defenses of marginalism). The dominant response was to breathe a sigh of relief: because there is a Darwinian mechanism operating in the background, we can stop worrying and go on with our optimizing models as usual. Milton Friedman (1953, p. 22) held that "given natural selection, acceptance of the [maximizing] hypothesis can be based largely on the judgment that it summarizes appropriately the conditions for survival." But there was another response, rarer and more interesting. If what really lies behind economic activity is some kind of selection mechanism, then perhaps we should pay much more attention to analyzing how that mechanism works.

---

[4]   Although, when pressed, they admitted that they deviated from markup pricing when competitive conditions dictated.

Box 7.1   How the zebra got its stripes

In his iconic collection of bedtime tales for children, *Just So Stories* (1902), Rudyard Kipling explained how the leopard got its spots. Originally possessed of a featureless brown-gray coat, the leopard discovered that his prey, giraffes and zebras, had become invisible to him as, the better to blend into new landscapes to which they had migrated, they adopted mottled coats. With help and prodding from a human, the leopard too adopted camouflage, which enabled him to lie in wait for his victims more effectively.

Clearly, this is a (fanciful) case of conscious optimization, not of evolution, even if it is implied that the trait of spots was subsequently passed down to later generations of leopards in some Lamarckian fashion. But the tale does illustrate the idea of *functionalism*: that we can explain a persistent feature by examining the function it serves. Spots were adopted, and they persisted, because they served the function of camouflage, which was valuable for the leopard.

This is in many ways an appealing idea, and various forms of (often nuanced) functionalism were at the heart of social theory in the middle of the twentieth century. But critics pointed to a problem that Kipling's tales illustrate starkly: it is far too easy to come up with a story to explain the function of something we observe. Indeed, this criticism of functionalism goes back at least to the eighteenth century and another famous teller of tales. In *Candide* (1759), Voltaire's Dr. Pangloss holds that "as all things have been created for some end, they must necessarily be created for the best end. Observe, for instance, the nose is formed for spectacles, therefore we wear spectacles."

Much – perhaps even all – of the economics of organization is about finding stories to explain the functions of the organizational and institutional structures we observe. Ultimately, we cannot do without functionalism. But the moral of this tale is that we need to avoid jumping to easy stories. As Karl Popper (1963) rightly argued, knowledge advances through the combination of conjecture and criticism. The lesson of Kipling and Voltaire is that conjecture is easy. But criticism is hard. Economists need to think carefully about the conjectures they put forward in explaining organizational form. More importantly, they need to engage in a process of constant criticism and revision of their explanations – and those of others.

This is also how evolutionary biology works. For example, Ruxton (2002) surveys the various conjectures about, and the evidence for, the benefits to zebras of having stripes. This is not an account of how the zebra *got* its stripes (Gould 1983). As in the economics of organization, the answer to the "how" question is evolution. But conjectures about the possible adaptive functions of stripes are an essential part of a specific account of the zebra.

In a comment on Alchian's selection argument, Penrose (1952, p. 812) pointed out that in biological evolution, selection operates on traits that can reproduce themselves. But in the story about drivers dispersing from Chicago, there is no reproduction. If another thousand drivers leave again the next day, they have retained no information from the previous day and are on average no better at finding gas stations than the drivers the day before. In an important sense, rational economic agents are also much like Alchian's drivers. They too have no persistence of memory; they take each day afresh as they search for a new optimal solution. But for selection to operate, there has to be at least some stickiness, some repetitiveness of behavior. As Sidney Winter (1971, p. 245) put it, "to make a 'natural selection' argument plausible in economics, some mechanism playing the role of genetic inheritance must be discovered."

An obvious candidate model, already long aired within social science, would be to suppose that economic agents follow rules. Rules are sticky almost by definition; and rules, or something very like them, might be a good candidate for the genetic element in an evolutionary story. In the 1950s and 1960s, the arrival of the digital computer made the rule-following model all the more salient. Influenced by the computer – and indeed interwoven with the field of computer science – the Carnegie School of Richard Cyert, James March, Herbert Simon and others proposed accounts of rule-like human behavior (Cyert and March 1963; March and Simon 1958). Simon (1956) famously argued that humans are subject to severe cognitive limitations that make it impossible for them constantly to optimize in any strong sense. Humans are "boundedly rational," Simon suggested, and as a result, they must often "satisfice" rather than optimize.[5] And satisficing typically means the following of rules in a world too complex for nonstop optimization.

---

[5]   I have always considered the term "bounded rationality" misleading (Langlois 1990), since it is cognitive capacity, not rationality, that is bounded. Cognitively bounded agents can still be rational in the sense of

Influenced by the Carnegie School, Richard Nelson and Sidney Winter painted a sophisticated portrait of an evolutionary approach to economics. In their account, both individual agents and organizations follow *routines*, which are rule-like forms of behavior. The forces of selection then operate on the routines, which serve as the analogue of genetic material: routines are genes (Nelson and Winter 1982, p. 15). Organizations thus appear as a collection of routines – of ways of doing things – that exist independently of the individual personnel who follow the routines.[6] An automobile assembly plant, for example, continues to operate – and learn – even as workers come and go (Levitt, List and Syverson 2013). For Nelson and Winter, routines are organizational memory, "the organizational analogue of individual skill" (Nelson and Winter 2002, p. 30). Like Richardson, they call these organizational skills *capabilities*.

With organizational capabilities (or, if you prefer, the routines that underlie them) as the genetic material, we can return to the idea of a selection mechanism – and we can begin to think about why it is worth examining the ongoing evolutionary process itself rather than just assuming its outcome. In the method of comparative-institutional analysis, we usually compare fully formed (perhaps ideal-typical) versions of the organizational alternatives. But as an evolutionary learning process unfolds, the alternatives are seldom fully formed; they are constantly morphing and reshaping. And we must sometimes study them not as final products of the evolutionary process but as out-of-equilibrium way stations (Langlois 1984).

In an evolutionary story, for one thing, "fitness" is a relative concept. A form need not be "optimal" in any absolute sense; it merely has to be good

---

behaving reasonably – doing the best they can with what they have and what they know.

[6] Like the concept of rational choice, the concept of routines is a subtle and often controverted one, and I cannot do justice to the topic here. Do individuals or organizations follow routines because they are programmed to do so? Or are routines about constraints that guide individuals and organizations along relatively stable paths, perhaps by taking some possible (rational) choices off the table? Geoffrey Hodgson (2023, p. 11) sees routines as "dispositions" to behave in a certain way in an organizational setting. He defines routines as "organizational capacities to produce conditional patterns of behavior within an organized group of individuals, involving sequential responses to cues."

enough.[7] One immediate implication is that the organizational form we observe depends on the strength of the selection environment. A weak selection environment will allow forms to survive that would have been eliminated in a stronger (or merely different) selection environment. Some have argued, for example, that the American automobile industry after World War II had evolved in an environment without significant international rivals, which left the industry vulnerable to Japanese competition at the end of the twentieth century.[8] As market shares fell precipitously, the American firms struggled without great success to acquire the manufacturing capabilities and to emulate the organizational structures that were making the Japanese industry successful.

The American firms found it hard to adapt because they possessed their own set of capabilities; acquired over a long period of time in a specific environment, these were sticky, complex, and interconnected. Here is another implication of taking the evolutionary metaphor seriously: the capabilities and structures an organization possesses will depend on its history. In fancier language, what we observe at any time may be *path dependent* – it may depend not on forces working at the time of observation but on factors that operated in the past. (Chapter 9 will consider the concept of path dependence more carefully.)

Just as an organizational structure we observe today may reflect factors from the past more than it does forces at work today, an organizational structure may also be influenced by unobserved beliefs and expectations about the future. For example, when technology is changing rapidly – such as perhaps telecommunications technology at the turn of the

---

[7] Which calls to mind another old joke. Two hikers are resting under a tree when they are suddenly menaced by a fierce grizzly bear. One of the hikers begins lacing up his shoes. "You don't think you can outrun that bear, do you?" says the other hiker. "I don't have to outrun the bear," his partner replies. "I just have to outrun you."

[8] "Hal Sperlich, possibly the most talented product man of his generation in Detroit, said that the earlier era was marked by what was virtually an illusion of competition and hard work but in truth was a competition within a protected zone, finally more about the changing of hemlines than anything else. He compared the old days to being the best tennis players in a pleasant suburban country club, aware that everyone else in the club watched their fast, smooth Sunday game. 'And then one day,' he said, speaking of the arrival of the Japanese, 'Bjorn Borg and John McEnroe walked on the court'" (Halberstam 1986, p. 46).

twenty-first century – we might observe firms integrated into a variety of businesses simply because no one could be sure which technology would win out in the future. If we attempted to analyze firm scope by thinking about the comparative advantages of firms versus market at that instance in time (or in some hypothetical equilibrium), we would get the wrong answer.

In a sense, we made a more specific version of this point earlier when thinking about incomplete contracts. Frank Knight (1921), arguably the (generally unacknowledged) progenitor of the incomplete-contracts view of the firm, held that it is the radical uncertainty of the future that explains the organization of firms.[9] Because of radical uncertainty (now often called "Knightian" uncertainty), it is people with a comparative advantage in judgment about the future who hold the ultimate decision rights in capitalist firms (more about the faculty of judgment in the next chapter). This is not how the world would be organized in a world without uncertainty; that would probably look more like the various failed schemes for socialist central planning, all of which were designed without uncertainty in mind.

Yet, as Alchian (1950) pointed out, an evolutionary theory would not start with perfect information and then add in uncertainty (as Knight did); it would start with complete ignorance and then add in knowledge through learning. We saw that relational contracts, which we observe both within the firm and across firms, are responses in the present to ignorance about the future. Agents enter into a relational contract as a way to respond flexibly by pushing decisions into a better-informed future. Robert Gibbons and Rebecca Henderson (2012) have effectively linked the idea of relational contracts to routines and capabilities. Such contracts demand mutual trust; but they also require gradual agreement among the partners about what is to be accomplished and how it is to be accomplished. In addition to commitment, they argue, a relational contract seeks *clarity*, a developing shared understanding of the rules of the game and the routines the participants are to follow. Clarity is not an input to a relational contract; it is an output.

---

[9]   By radical uncertainty here, I mean not only uncertainty about states of the world within a known framework, what I like to call *parametric uncertainty*, but also uncertainty about what states of the world are even possible, what I call *structural uncertainty* (Langlois 1984).

What is the bottom line? We need to take both the evolutionary process and the idea of capabilities seriously in explaining organizational form. Sometimes we observe organizational form A not because it won the Coasean horse race on a level playing field, but because – for the moment at least – it is winning a race on a twisting and muddy field.

This perspective has long suggested to me that we need a way to think about organization in an uncertain and changing environment. Because capabilities can usually be acquired only slowly over time, we cannot run a horse race that presumes organizations – or markets – already have the necessary capabilities at hand. Sometimes, of course, capabilities (or, rather, their services) can be bought readily on a market. But, especially in the face of change and innovation, new capabilities must often be called into existence at a cost. Those costs – the (opportunity) costs of not having the capabilities you need when you need them – are what I call *dynamic transaction costs* (Langlois 1992).

In the early twentieth century, the Ford Motor Company became the poster child for vertical integration, especially with the completion of the massive River Rouge plant. Oliver Williamson (1985, p. 119) viewed much of this as "mistaken integration": integration that, he was sure, a competitive selection process would eventually weed out. And, indeed, after World War II Ford began to divest itself of its founder's wilder forays into vertical integration, including a Brazilian rubber plantation and considerable ore holdings (Nevins and Hill 1962, p. 323). Yet if we look closer at the core business of Ford Motor Company, beginning with its development of the moving assembly line at its Highland Park plant, we see vertical integration that was arguably both efficient and motivated by dynamic transaction costs (Langlois and Robertson 1989). Because the Ford team was at the cutting edge of making parts finely adapted to the Model T, it was often cheaper to manufacture equipment in-house than for the company's engineers to explain to outsiders what was needed.[10] More importantly, the Ford engineers frequently didn't immediately

---

[10]   A widely repeated, if perhaps apocryphal, anecdote illustrates the point. Ford engineer Charles Sorenson "recalled that when Charles Morgana sent out specifications for a Ford-designed machine tool to machine tool manufacturers, the latter often came back to Morgana saying that there must have been an error because the machine could not do what it was supposed to do. Morgana would then show the tool builders that no mistake had been made because the Ford-designed and Ford-built prototype could indeed turn out the specified number of units within the specified

know what they needed. They were experimenting and trying new things; and being able to survey the entire operation systemically often led to unexpected improvements.

If all production knowledge were explicit and encoded in blueprints, it should never be costly to inform and persuade outside suppliers. Indeed, innovators should always be concerned only with protecting their ideas, which could easily slip out to competitors at zero marginal cost.[11] As Morris Silver pointed out, however, in the real world quite the opposite is often the case. The innovator's "problem is that he cannot, at reasonable cost, convey his implausible 'secret' to those with the technical capabilities needed to produce the required operations at the lowest cost. Finding himself unable to secure the cooperation of the latter producers, the entrepreneur must direct his finite managerial resources into areas for which he does not have a comparative advantage. This in fact reduces the profitability of his innovation" (Silver 1984, p. 17).

In some instances, then, dynamic transaction costs imply vertical integration. But in other cases, they can lead to vertical *disintegration*. If we start with a world of market transactions, internal organization may sometimes be a speedier way to deal with economic change, especially radical or systemic change. But if we start with a world of internal organization, dynamic transaction costs may make vertical disintegration a cheaper alternative.

The work of Steven Klepper (2016) provides some good examples. In his careful, detailed study – what he called nanoeconomics – of technological change in a number of industries, he showed the importance to economic growth of *spinoffs*. Especially in a regime of rapid technological advance, employees within existing firms often perceive opportunities to do things differently or to take the technology in a new direction, perhaps a more specialized direction. But, just as Silver's market entrepreneurs find it costly to persuade transaction partners, Klepper's internal entrepreneurs find it costly to persuade managers to take up their ideas. Indeed, given the existing matrix of capabilities within the firm, the

---

limits of precision. 'So it went with the thousand pieces of machinery that we bought,' concluded Sorensen" (Hounshell 1984, p. 231).

[11]   And this might be a motive for vertical integration, to the extent that integration is a cheaper or more effective alternative for protecting slippery ideas than intellectual property rights (Teece 1986).

managers may be right to say no. So, assuming market-supporting institutions (like financial markets) are robust enough, the internal entrepreneur strikes off on his or her own to start a new firm. Klepper goes so far as to argue that it is spinoffs, not Marshallian external economies per se, that explain the phenomenon of industrial districts like Silicon Valley or Detroit in the early years of the auto industry.

Suggested readings

Robert Gibbons and Rebecca Henderson, "Relational Contracts and Organizational Capabilities," *Organization Science* **23**(5): 1350–1364, 2012.

Richard N. Langlois, "Transaction Cost Economics in Real Time," *Industrial and Corporate Change* **1**(1): 99–127, 1992.

Richard R. Nelson and Sidney G. Winter, *An Evolutionary Theory of Economic Change*. Cambridge: Harvard University Press, 1982, especially Chapters 4 and 5.

G. B. Richardson, "The Organisation of Industry," *The Economic Journal* **82**(327): 883–896, 1972.

8 Cognitive comparative advantage and the organization of work

In the most famous scene from Charlie Chaplin's 1936 film *Modern Times*, the Little Tramp character finds himself working at an assembly line. As each subassembly comes down the conveyor, the Tramp has to tighten a nut with a large wrench and pass the assembly on. He must do this over and over again, at the speed of the assembly line. (Needless to say, all does not go well.) This way of organizing work would not have surprised Adam Smith. As we saw in Chapter 1, the division of labor operates by specializing workers to tasks. With increases in the extent of the market, subdivision becomes finer and finer – and tasks become simpler and simpler.

We need look no further than Smith himself for the negative implications of such an increasingly fine division of labor: "The man whose whole life is spent in performing a few simple operations, of which the effects are perhaps always the same, or very nearly the same, has no occasion to exert his understanding or to exercise his invention in finding out expedients for removing difficulties which never occur. He naturally loses, therefore, the habit of such exertion, and generally becomes as stupid and ignorant as it is possible for a human creature to become" (Smith 1976 [1776], V.i.178).

Following a long tradition of radical thought, Stephen Marglin (1974) went further, arguing that capitalists had deliberately imposed this mode of work organization, not because the division of labor is more efficient than crafts production but because by *deskilling* tasks the capitalists could take away the workers' potential for economic rents, turning labor into the mass army of undifferentiated laborers predicted by Marx.[1]

---

[1]   "Intelligence in production expands in one direction, because it vanishes in many others. What is lost by the detail labourers, is concentrated

For many, notably those intent on criticizing capitalist work organization, this is nearly the end of the story. In fact, however, it is actually much nearer to the middle of the story. Recall Smith's assumptions. Tools start out specialized to the various activities involved in production, but labor is unspecialized. The division of labor consists in matching the specialization of labor to that of machines. But this doesn't exhaust the possibilities. Why can't *machines* change their level of specialization?

Following Ames and Rosenberg (1965), define the width of a *skill* as the number of activities an operative or machine engages in. Clearly, a crafts artisan is more skilled in this sense than an assembly-line worker. Define *specialization* as the reciprocal of skill: the number of doers (humans or machines) per activity. By this definition, specialization ranges between 0 (complete non-specialization) and 1 (complete specialization). Now consider a production process involving exactly three activities (a_1, a_2, a_3). (See Figure 8.1.) Technology A is what we have called crafts production. One worker undertakes all three activities, but machines — which are clearly *tools* in this case — are specialized to activities. Technology B is what Smith had in mind: workers and tools are equally specialized to activities. Technology C is the forgotten alternative: workers are specialized, but machines — and now they are indeed *machines* not just tools — become less specialized.

Machines have become less specialized in the sense that a single device has taken over — has automated — all three stages of production. Many thinkers have conceptualized automation as a natural extension of the division of labor: each worker wields specialized tools, and automation is just a matter of hooking the relevant tools together (and typically connecting them to inanimate power so that they run by themselves.)[2] As we will see, however, creating skilled machines typically involves redesigning the work process, often in a radical way, so that it meets the needs of

---

in the capital that employs them" (Marx 1961 [1887], Volume 1, Part IV, Chapter XIV, p. 361).

[2]   Take Charles Babbage, for example: "When each process has been reduced to the use of some simple tool, the union of all these tools, actuated by one moving power, constitutes a machine" (Babbage 1846, Chapter 19, Paragraph 225). Similarly, Karl Marx, who probably got the idea from Babbage: "The machine proper is therefore a mechanism that, after being set in motion, performs with its tools the same operations that were formerly done by the workman with similar tools" (Marx 1961 [1887], Volume 1, Part IV, Chapter XIV, p. 374).

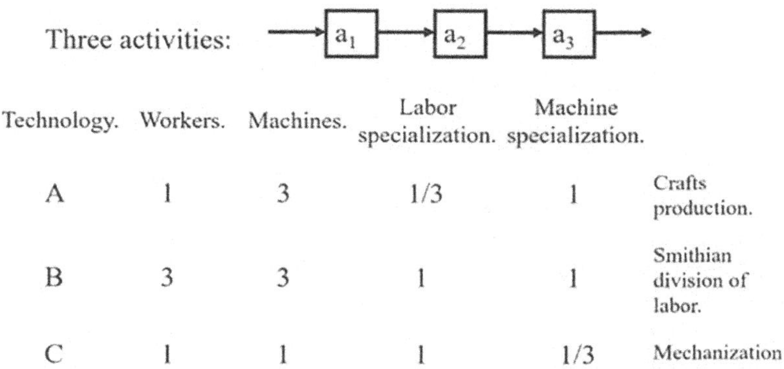

Technology.	Workers.	Machines.	Labor specialization.	Machine specialization.	
A	1	3	1/3	1	Crafts production.
B	3	3	1	1	Smithian division of labor.
C	1	1	1	1/3	Mechanization

Figure 8.1   Labor and machine specialization

what we might call machine cognition. Mechanization is not merely a robotic version of the human division of labor.

Smith tells us that growth in the extent of the market drives the progressive transition from Technology A to Technology B. But such growth also, and perhaps more importantly, drives a transition from Technology B to Technology C, which we can understand as a further manifestation of the larger division of labor with which Smith was concerned.

Smith describes the manufacture of pins in his era, in which ten men, organized according to principles of the division of labor, could make about 48,000 pins a day, or almost 5,000 per person per day. By Marx's era, making pins was already the business of machines, and a single machine could crank out 145,000 a day. One woman or girl could supervise four machines, which means almost 600,000 per person per day (Marx 1961 [1887], Volume 1, Part IV, Chapter XV, Section 8, p. 460). As of 1980, one person could supervise 24 machines, each making 500 pins a minute, or about 6 million pins per person per day (Pratten 1980). That's a two orders of magnitude increase in productivity in the first century as machines replaced the division of hand labor but only(!) a single order of magnitude increase in productivity over the next century as machines improved.

A similar transition from the division of labor to mechanization took place in the making of matches, which you can see illustrated dramatically by visiting the Match Museum in the town of Jönköping, Sweden, which was the "match capital of the world" for much of the nineteenth and early twentieth centuries. In the beginning, the industry took precisely the form Smith predicted. Cottagers in the town and surrounding countryside assumed a variety of subdivided tasks, from chopping and cutting the match wood to folding and gluing matchboxes to the debilitating and ultimately gruesome task of coating the tips with chemicals.[3] But it was mechanization, not a finer subdivision of putting-out tasks, that thrust Jönköping to prominence in the match industry. In 1844, the brothers Johan and Carl Lundström opened a factory in Jönköping to capitalize on the recently invented safety match, improvements to which Johan had just patented. In 1870, they hired the inventor Alexander Lagerman to further mechanize the process of making matches. Lagerman's machines not only assumed the tasks of humans but, more significantly, combined within their operations what had been previously many separate tasks, and they did so in a way that often differed dramatically from the unmechanized sequence of tasks.

Box 8.1   Telephone switching

Telephone switching is a good example of a set of sensory coordination tasks to which humans are cognitively well adapted. In the early decades of the telephone, a customer would make a connection by speaking to a human operator, almost always a young woman, who would plug the customer's line into the appropriate jack. The problem, of course, is that this technology doesn't scale well: if you need twice as much switching, you need twice as many operators. Since the number of possible connections in a telephone network rises quadratically with the number of users, this is a problem. Already by the 1920s, 60 percent of the 215,000 people working in the US telephone industry were operators; by 1930, there were 190,000 telephone operators in the US (Feigenbaum and Gross 2024a).

Mechanization was the solution. But mechanization did not, and could not, replicate the task sequence of human-centric switching. It required a complete redesign of the task structure of the telephone system. Because of the complex and interdependent character of the system, which had been designed around human switching,

---

[3]   Which produced phosphorus necrosis in the workers. The transition to the safety match after 1844 had the happy effect of substituting less toxic red phosphorus for the more dangerous yellow phosphorus.

mechanization took nearly a century (Feigenbaum and Gross 2024b). Mechanized switching had been invented in the 1880s; the last human operator was not replaced until 1978. Although the incumbent operators suffered unemployment, the new technology did not reduce overall human employment, and the loss of operator jobs was counterbalanced by jobs, including wholly new categories of work, in other areas of telephony (Feigenbaum and Gross 2024a).

Significantly, human cognition could not be eliminated from the system entirely. For one thing, some components of what had once been the work of the operator needed to be offloaded onto the customer. In the old days, you merely had to pick up the receiver and say, "Mabel, get me George down to the hardware store." With the new mechanical system, by contrast, you had to find or remember a series of digits associated with George's Hardware and then dial it yourself with an eye-brain-hand sequence. Simple as this now sounds, AT&T executives at the time fretted that customers would lack the cognitive capacity to keep the phone number in mind between the time they looked it up in the directory (itself a new part of the task structure) and the time they finished spinning the phone's dial (Lipartito 1994, p. 1105). Fortunately, operators had long used the mnemonic device of giving memorable names to exchanges, like the Walnut exchange in my childhood household; and by assigning letters to numbers, the phone company could pass this mnemonic along to its cognitively challenged customers. Of course, nowadays you can once again just say, "Siri, dial George's Hardware," even if you are more likely to log on to the company's website, where you can execute a complex set of tasks that obviates having to chat with George in the first place.

If mechanization takes tasks entirely out of the hands of workers, are we left to infer that the progress of mechanization will inevitably consign humans to Marx's immiserated proletarian army of the unskilled and unemployed? Joel Mokyr and other economic historians have pointed out that the fear of technological unemployment has a long history — and that the fear has always proven ill founded (Mokyr, Vickers and Ziebarth 2015). Although machines can certainly substitute for human labor, mechanization also increases productivity, which in turn increases output and thereby calls forth additional human labor. Machines can sometimes be complements to labor rather than substitutes. Notice that in Figure 8.1, the degree of labor specialization in Technology C is 1. There is one human who is specialized in tending the machine, broadly understood to include programming, maintaining, or even improving it. And that complex set of tasks is complementary to mechanization.

Today, of course, so-called artificial intelligence seems to be taking over tasks that are far more complex, and perhaps far more "human," than those on the Tramp's assembly line. (If you don't believe me, just ask Alexa or Siri.) Perhaps this time will be different, many wonder; perhaps this time the specter of technological unemployment will finally come for us.

In 1960, the editors of a collected volume challenged Herbert Simon to answer this question: "The Corporation: Will It Be Managed by Machines?" In this marvelous but long-neglected paper, Simon articulated his vision of what the "knowledge economy" of the future — 1985! — would look like. Perhaps surprisingly for someone given to the most strident predictions of the speedy and inevitable success of artificial intelligence, Simon is clear that we should not expect computers (or machines more generally) to replace humans in all occupations. As David Ricardo taught long ago, what matters is not the absolute level of skill (whether wide or deep) that machines attain relative to humans but rather the *comparative advantages* of machines relative to humans.

> Man's comparative advantage in energy production has been greatly reduced in most situations – to the point where he is no longer a significant source of power in our economy. He has been supplanted also in performing many relatively simple and repetitive eye-brain-hand sequences. He has retained his greatest comparative advantage in: (1) the use of his brain as a flexible general-purpose problem-solving device, (2) the flexible use of his sensory organs and hands, and (3) the use of his legs, on rough terrain as well as smooth, to make this general-purpose sensing-thinking-manipulating system available wherever it is needed. (Simon 1960, p. 31.)

The implication is that with growth in the extent of the market, we should see humans crowded into tasks that call for the kinds of cognition for which humans have been equipped by biological evolution. These human cognitive abilities range from the exercise of judgment in situations of ambiguity and surprise to more mundane abilities in spatio-temporal perception and locomotion.[4] By contrast, we should see machines

---

[4]   A less well-known bit in *Modern Times* illustrates this point. After his stint on the assembly line, the Little Tramp is selected as the guinea pig

(increasingly computers) crowded into tasks that require the following of explicit rules.

Production under the division of labor is importantly a matter of coordination among tasks. Coordination means that each stage must somehow do the right things at the right time: each stage must make decisions that are appropriate in light of the decisions that came before and will come after. A craft artisan is constantly interacting with and fiddling with the process of production at each step. But when labor is more finely divided, parts become standardized, and much of the coordination among stages is designed into the process itself. Such hard-wired coordination is limited by the complexity and unpredictability of the environment. If a square hole awaits on the assembly line, the production process will work smoothly only if what arrives is always a square peg — and never a round peg, let alone a whale or a bowl of petunias. Indeed, the higher the throughput of a production system, the more vulnerable the system is to spurious variation. If a round peg appears when a square one is wanted, the entire system may come to a crashing halt.

Box 8.2   Knowledge reuse

In a deep sense, standardization is the secret sauce that accounts for the efficiency of the division of labor relative to crafts production and, perhaps even more dramatically, of mechanization. The reason is that standardization is a mechanism of *knowledge reuse*. In effect, standardization means that operatives (including mechanical ones) do not have to expend resources to process information about each unit produced; they can instead learn once and apply that knowledge over and over again to more and more units. Indeed, I would go so far as to argue that the reuse of knowledge is the principal source of economies of scale in production (Langlois 1999).

With a reduction in uncertainty — permitting an increase in standardization — a particular sequence of activities can be hard-wired into a production system or machine.

---

for a new machine that automatically feeds a worker lunch. Here too, hilarity ensues. But the humor emerges largely from the viewer's recognition of the absurdity of trying to mechanize spatio-temporal tasks that are far easier for humans to do for themselves than for machines to do for them.

> In drilling the plate A without the jig the skilled mechanic must expend *thought* as well as skill in properly locating the holes. The unskilled operator need expend no thought regarding the location of the holes. That part of the mental labor has been done once for all by the tool maker. It appears, therefore, that a "transfer of thought" or intelligence can also be made from a person to a machine. If the quantity of parts to be made is sufficiently large to justify the expenditure, it is possible to make machines to which all the required skill and thought have been transferred and the machine does not require even an attendant, except to make adjustments. Such machines are known as full automatic machines. (Kimball 1929, p. 26, emphasis original)

As this quote from an old text on the organization of industry suggests, the transfer to a machine of "intelligence" often takes the form of a jig, pattern, or die. And, as Armen Alchian (1959) pointed out in his sadly neglected reconstruction of the neoclassical cost function, the "method of production is a function of the volume of output, especially when output is produced from basic dies — and there are few, if any, methods of production that do not involve 'dies'" (Alchian 1959, p. 29). As the volume of output increases, it pays to invest in more durable dies. For example, if, in the old days of paper, you wanted to run off a few copies of a memo, a mimeograph machine would have done the trick. If you needed several hundred copies of documents on an ongoing basis, it might have been worth investing in a small offset press. For even larger predictable production runs, it would have paid to bring in a more serious printing press. As volume and predictability of output call forth greater "durability of dies," unit costs decline.

This point is worth remembering, as some Principles of Economics textbooks have traditionally illustrated the concept of economies of scale with what is actually a special case and a red herring: the volume of a pipe or a warehouse grows as the cube of the length, whereas the surface area of the pipe or warehouse, and therefore the materials needed to build it, grows as the square of the length.

As Simon tells us, there are fundamentally only two ways to deal with an unpredictable environment. "If we want an organism or mechanism to behave effectively in a complex and changing environment, we can design into it adaptive mechanisms that allow it to respond flexibly to the demands the environment places on it. Alternatively, we can try to simplify and stabilize the environment. We can adapt organism to environment or environment to organism" (Simon 1960, p. 33). Consider the problem of crossing rough terrain, like most of the American continent in the early nineteenth century. Like the Native Americans before them, the earliest Western explorers used Simon's first technique: they took advantage of the adaptive mechanism of the human locomotion system. They walked and climbed, at least when there weren't suitable rivers available. But once a larger population began gravitating west, it became worthwhile to use the second approach. A steam locomotive is a high-throughput transportation system that works phenomenally well so long as one first prepares the environment to reduce variation almost to zero. So the railroad companies altered the terrain — they laid tracks — to accommodate this high-speed, high-volume, but inflexible technology.

An assembly line is like a railroad. It increases throughput by eliminating variation, thus making itself vulnerable to whatever variation remains. It is for this reason that such systems need to *buffer* environmental influences (Thompson 1967, p. 20) by placing human information processors between the uncertainty and the high-throughput production process. At the same time that the assembly line "deskills" workers by making their tasks simpler and more routine, it also surrounds those workers (or the machines that inevitably take on the simplest and and most routine tasks) with a large number of more flexible (more widely skilled) workers at multiple levels, from maintenance workers to top management (Stinchcombe 1990, p. 64). Uncertainty and variation can never be eliminated; at best, they can be pushed "up the hierarchy" to be dealt with by adaptable and less-specialized humans.

These human "buffers" are information-processing systems that mediate between a complex and uncertain environment and the system in need of predictability. Human cognition can often interpret complex data from the external world and translate that data into the kinds of routine information the productive system can use (Stinchcombe 1990). For example, a professor translates the complex information on an essay exam into a letter grade that the Registrar's office can process; a court translates the complex proceedings of a trial into a dichotomous verdict; a physician translates the complex inputs from observation and medical instrumentation into a diagnosis, which results in a relatively unambiguous set of instructions for nurses, pharmacists, patients, etc.

Frank Knight understood this long ago. "In industrial life," he wrote, "purely routine operations are inevitably taken over by machinery. The duties of the machine tender may seem mechanical and uniform, but they are really not so throughout the operation. His function is to complete the carrying-out of the process to the point where it becomes entirely uniform so that the machine can take hold of it, or else to begin with the uniform output of the machine and start it on the way of diversification. Some part of the task will practically always be found to require conscious judgment, which is to say the meeting of uncertainty, the exercise of responsibility, in the ordinary sense of these terms" (Knight 1921, III.X.7, pp. 294–295).

Except for a few economic historians (like Ames and Rosenberg), until recently economists had abandoned Adam Smith's task approach to labor economics in favor of the production function, which blurs any distinctions between the services supplied by capital and those supplied by labor. In the twenty-first century, however, David Autor and his coauthors – explicitly influenced by Simon's 1960 paper – have returned to the task approach and developed it into a thriving, cutting-edge branch of labor economics (Autor 2013; Autor, Levy and Murnane 2003). Like Simon, Autor and his colleagues distinguish between routine tasks, which require the following of explicit rules, and non-routine or abstract tasks, which require imagination, judgment in the sense of Frank Knight, and often tacit knowledge in the sense of Michael Polanyi (Autor 2014).

It is true that, with the continued fall in the relative price of computation power and the development of so-called artificial intelligence – prediction systems using big data – many tasks once assumed to require advanced human-style cognition can, in fact, be reengineered as a system of rules and assigned to computers. But short of the "singularity," the fabled point at which computers become self-aware, it will not be the case that machines will take all human jobs.[5] This is implied in the very idea of comparative advantage.

Ultimately, the problem many fear is not the complete displacement of humans by machines but rather that as people lose comparative advantage in physical labor and simple rule-following tasks, human skills are becoming crowded into the extremes of the occupational distribution,

---

[5] The idea of the singularity is often attributed to the late mathematician and science fiction author Vernor Vinge (1993).

with highly remunerative jobs requiring analytic reasoning and problem solving at one end and less-remunerative in-person service jobs at the other end (Acemoglu and Autor 2012; Autor 2013, p. 189). Precisely because they often involve simple rule-following tasks, the jobs of people with low levels of formal human capital, notably workers in manufacturing, are most vulnerable to displacement by machines. Workers idled by machines will shift into jobs comprising tasks that require human-style cognition. That means service jobs like cleaners, hairdressers, waitresses, personal-care workers, and (for the moment) truck drivers. But these are not likely to be more remunerative than their old manufacturing jobs (all other things equal), since there is generally an abundant supply of workers without a high level of human capital who are capable of filling such jobs. By contrast, the jobs that are complementary to technology typically require high levels of formal human capital, which is expensive to acquire and therefore relatively scarce and remunerative.

In the end, however, it is an empirical question which jobs will be substitutes for machine cognition and which will be complements to it. As Autor (2024) has more recently speculated, it may well turn out that AI will in fact augment the skills of those with lower levels of human capital, enabling them to undertake many tasks that are today the province of highly trained experts. We know that in activities like medical diagnosis and even chess, humans and computers working together can outperform either humans by themselves or computers by themselves[6] (Agrawal, Gans and Goldfarb 2018, p. 65; Brynjolfsson and McAfee 2014, pp. 189–190). The complementarity, and the advantage, appear to come from the division of labor within the team: machines can do the parts that require high-speed rule following and humans can do the parts that require what Knight called judgment. With skill-augmenting AI as a teammate, many workers, including those with less formal training, may in the end be able to enter realms of better-paying occupations that had previously been foreclosed to them.

Suggested readings

Edward Ames and Nathan Rosenberg, "The Progressive Division and Specialization of Industries," *The Journal of Development Studies* 1(4): 363–383, 1965.

---

[6]   But for a counterexample, see Agarwal et al. (2023).

David H. Autor, "The 'Task Approach' to Labor Markets: An Overview," *Journal for Labour Market Research* **46**(3): 185–199, 2013.
David H. Autor, "Applying AI to Rebuild Middle Class Jobs," National Bureau of Economic Research Working Paper Series No. 32140, February 2024.
Richard N. Langlois, "Cognitive Comparative Advantage and the Organization of Work: Lessons from Herbert Simon's Vision of the Future," *Journal of Economic Psychology* **24**(2): 167–187, 2003.

9 Modular systems

In many ways, this book has been a conversation between Adam Smith and Ronald Coase. From Smith, we took a concern with the structure and organization of tasks in the economy. From Coase, we took a concern with the costs of transacting, that is, with the costs of moving resources, including information, among tasks. In the end, however, these two concerns are really aspects of a single larger concern. The division of labor (along with its complement, mechanization) is a manifestation of increased complexity in society; transaction costs are about how that complexity is managed. Both are aspects of the design of *complex systems*.

To help think about complex systems, we need to return to another of our interlocutors, Herbert Simon. Simon described a complex system as "one made up of a large number of parts that interact in a nonsimple way. In such systems the whole is more than the sum of the parts, not in an ultimate, metaphysical sense but in the important pragmatic sense that, given the properties of the parts and the laws of their interaction, it is not a trivial matter to infer the properties of the whole" (Simon 1962, p. 468). Complexity is thus a matter both of the sheer number of distinct parts the system comprises and of the nature of the interconnections or interdependencies among those parts. In this chapter, we will eventually want to think about the parts of the complex system as *tasks* and the interdependencies among them as *transactions*.

The problem with complexity, of course, is that as the parts multiply, the system is in danger of becoming an unmanageable spaghetti tangle. It is also in danger of becoming unstable. Local actions may well affect ramify to distant parts of the system in unintended and unforeseeable ways. As Jeff Goldblum's supercilious mathematician put it in the 1993 film *Jurassic Park*, "a butterfly can flap its wings in Peking, and in Central Park you get rain instead of sunshine." If we change or interfere with the system, even in what may seem an insignificant manner, we do so at our peril.

In the mid-1960s, IBM introduced the 360 series of computers. This was a major departure for the company in computer design, and it would become a major landmark in the history of computing. Since its beginnings in the nineteenth century, as we have seen, IBM had thrived by using a relatively stable inventory of slowly improving parts to assemble bespoke information-technology solutions for customers[1] (Usselman 1993). The introduction of electronic technology did not initially change this model, but soon the problem of multiplying software products introduced a complexity bottleneck. IBM responded by radically transforming from a purveyor of bespoke architectures to the designer of a single stable architecture – the System 360 – that could be adapted to customer problems through standardized software and by mixing and matching standardized subassemblies.

From the point of view of hardware, the IBM 360 would be a *modular system* (Baldwin and Clark 2000, pp. 169–194). But the operating system – the 360's overarching control program – was another matter. The manager of the operating system project, Fred Brooks, insisted on a conscious attention to all interdependencies and a high level of communication among all participants. This included the creation and maintenance of a formal project workbook that documented every aspect of the system so that, in principle at least, every worker could determine how changes elsewhere would affect his or her part of the project. Brooks decided "that each programmer should see all the material, i.e., should have a copy of the workbook in his own office" (Brooks 1975, p. 76). But within six months there was one small problem. "The workbook was about five feet thick! If we had stacked up the 100 copies serving programmers in our offices in Manhattan's Time-Life Building, they would have towered above the building itself. Furthermore, the daily change distributions averaged two inches, some 150 pages to be interfiled in the whole. Maintenance of the workbook began to take a significant time from each workday" (Brooks 1975, p. 77). The team soon switched to microfiche. And, clearly, with modern technology, the workbook could reside online and be updated rapidly. But it was obvious that in the end this approach was entirely unworkable.

In his telling of this story, Brooks briefly considers but dismisses a "radical" alternative proposed by David Parnas, whose "thesis is that the

---

[1]   An example of what, following Henderson and Clark (1990), we will soon call *architectural innovation*.

programmer is most effective if shielded from, rather than exposed to the details of construction of system parts other than his own" (Brooks 1975, p. 78). Parnas (1972) is the inventor of the notion of *information hiding*, a key concept in the modern object-oriented approach to computer programming. Programmers had long understood the importance of breaking programs into manageable pieces. But genuine modularity requires more, since one can easily break a system into "modules" whose internal workings remain highly interdependent with the internal workings of other modules. Parnas argued that, especially in large projects, programmers should abandon designs based on simple flow charts and pay attention instead to minimizing interdependencies. If knowledge is hidden or *encapsulated* within a module, that knowledge cannot affect other parts of a system. Under this scheme, every module "is characterized by its knowledge of a design decision which it hides from all others. Its interface or definition was chosen to reveal as little as possible about its inner workings" (Parnas 1972, p. 1056).

Parnas's object-oriented approach to programming harkens back to what Simon (1962) called *decomposability*. Consider Figure 9.1. An entry of x in location a_{ij} means that element a_i communicates with element a_j. Matrix A is a non-decomposable system: every element communicates with every other element. That means that the behavior of every element potentially affects, and is potentially affected by, the behavior of every other element. It is the property of non-decomposability that accounts for high coordination costs and unforeseen and perhaps destabilizing interaction effects in a complex system. By contrast, Matrix B is a decomposable system. Communication is encapsulated within clusters of elements – modules – that do not communicate with elements "far away."

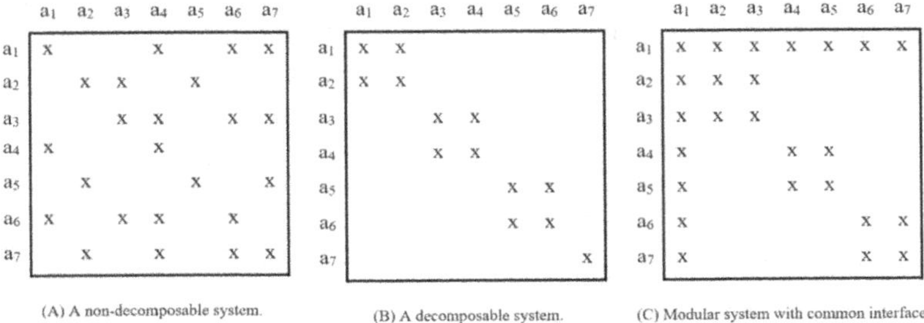

	a_1	a_2	a_3	a_4	a_5	a_6	a_7
a_1	x			x		x	x
a_2		x	x		x		
a_3			x	x		x	x
a_4	x			x			
a_5		x			x		x
a_6	x		x	x		x	
a_7		x		x		x	x

(A) A non-decomposable system.

	a_1	a_2	a_3	a_4	a_5	a_6	a_7
a_1	x	x					
a_2	x	x					
a_3			x	x			
a_4			x	x			
a_5					x	x	
a_6					x	x	
a_7							x

(B) A decomposable system.

	a_1	a_2	a_3	a_4	a_5	a_6	a_7
a_1	x	x	x	x	x	x	x
a_2	x	x	x				
a_3	x	x	x				
a_4	x			x	x		
a_5	x			x	x		
a_6	x					x	x
a_7	x					x	x

(C) Modular system with common interface.

Figure 9.1   Decomposable and modular systems

Notice, however, that, although a decomposable system like Matrix B clearly solves the problem of coordination, it does so by creating autarkic clusters: it eliminates the costs of cooperation by the expedient of eliminating cooperation between clusters (though not within clusters). The term modular system takes on many meanings in the literature, but one important candidate definition is that a modular system is a nearly decomposable system that preserves the possibility of universal cooperation by adopting a common interface (Langlois and Garzarelli 2008). The common interface enables, but also governs and disciplines, the communication among subsystems. In terms of Figure 9.1, an interface would be a set of elements that communicates with most or all the other elements. In Matrix C, element a_1 is the common interface: a_1 communicates with all the a_{ij} and all the a_{ij} communicate with a_1. In other respects, however, Matrix C remains sparse off the diagonal. The modules communicate with each other only through the interface, never directly.

Sparseness of the off-diagonal – what we might think of as the *leanness* of the system – is a crucial characteristic of a well-designed modular system.[2] The basic idea is that "system details that are likely to change independently should be the secrets of separate modules; the only assumptions that should appear in the interfaces between modules are those that are considered unlikely to change" (Parnas, Clemens and Weiss 1985, p. 260). Crucial to this schema are the ideas of *encapsulation* and *information hiding*. Not only do the parts not need to communicate extensively with one another, they are structurally *forbidden* from communicating with one another. In the language of Baldwin and Clark (2000), although the *visible design rules* of the system are common knowledge, each module must maintain its own *hidden design parameters*.

The hardware of the IBM 360 was a modular system with standardized interfaces between components, which enabled the rise of external makers of components, like plotters, memory storage devices, and even central processing units, that were "plug compatible" with the 360. Similarly,

---

[2] This idea has, in fact, been formalized mathematically. Modularity involves "a statistically surprising arrangement of edges," and, somewhat loosely put, the degree of modularity of a system can be measured by comparing the system's "edges" with "an equivalent network with edges placed at random" (Newman 2006, p. 8578). There is a deep relationship between modularity – and organization more generally – and the concept of low entropy (or non-randomness) in cybernetics (Langlois and Garrouste 1997).

with the advent of the IBM PC in the early 1980s, the microcomputer became a modular system with a relatively fixed (or at least slowly changing) architecture, interfaces, and standards (Langlois and Robertson 1992, pp. 301–302). Because of this standardization and the slowly changing character of the PC's basic structure, the industry experienced a phenomenal increase in value and reduction in cost arising almost entirely from improvements in modules (microprocessors, software, modems, peripherals, etc.) rather than from improvements in the way the modules connect together.

Baldwin and Clark argue that modular innovation of this sort excels for two basic reasons: modularity creates *options* and modular designs can *evolve*. A modular design creates options – so-called *real options*, analogous to those in the financial realm – in the sense that each module constitutes a kind of experiment (Baldwin and Clark 2000, pp. 159–160). One can exercise an option on a successful experiment but needn't exercise the option if the experiment doesn't pan out. Because modules can be swapped in and out with ease, a successful experiment can be swapped in and a failed (or less successful) experiment can be swapped out. If these experiments are fully uncorrelated with one another, they constitute a portfolio of options with benefits analogous to those of a fully diversified portfolio of assets. In this sense, through swapping better modules for inferior ones, the modular design is also evolving.

Baldwin and Clark are concerned principally with the conscious design of artifacts by humans, even as they view human design and Darwinian processes as fundamentally similar (Baldwin and Clark 2000, pp. 221–230). Herbert Simon went so far as to suggest that we should observe modular designs in nature because modular designs would have superior survival value. Thus, the famous parable of the watchmakers (Simon 1962, pp. 470–471). Tempus and Hora each made complex watches of some 1,000 pieces. Tempus made his watches as a single non-decomposable system, so when he had to put the work down to deal with a phone call from a customer, the whole thing fell apart, and he had to start over from scratch. By contrast, Hora made his watches out of stable modular subassemblies, so when he was interrupted, only one subassembly fell apart. Hora could thus make many more watches and was far more successful. The implication is that a nearly decomposable system is more robust to exogenous shocks.

But what does this parable really tell us about evolvability in a Darwinian system? True enough, the point of evolution is that an organism survives if it is able to withstand the buffets of its environment. If the environment changes, Darwinian processes will select for organisms that better fit the new environment. But, even in a world of punctuated equilibria, that evolutionary process may well mean the accretion of changes to the original form, not a full-scale system redesign. The result could be a well-adapted complex system made up of parts that are highly interdependent with one another. For example, the aerodynamics of the flight of a bird is a system with far more non-linear interactions than the aerodynamics of the flight of an airplane (Holland 2012, pp. 22–23). Unlike many precursors who had tried to pattern mechanical flight on the flapping of bird wings, the Wright brothers succeeded because they made their plane more modular than evolved birds by decoupling the system of propulsion from the system of control.[3] Biological evolution had not needed, and had not produced, that kind of modular design.

There is also evidence that non-modular architectures can often outperform modular ones in many highly demanding settings (Christensen, Verlinden and Westerman 2002). If the phone calls that so discombobulated Tempus were extremely rare events, Hora would not be at an advantage – and might have been at a disadvantage if Tempus's interdependent system could fine-tune a more accurate watch by taking advantage of connections within the system that Hora's design would have forbidden. In a sense, by restricting communication to the interface, a modular system may be leaving some stable-environment gains from trade on the table. As Brooks pointed out in criticizing the Parnasian approach to software, "a good information system both exposes interface errors and stimulates their correction" (Brooks 1975, p. 78). To the extent that a non-modular system tends to reveal errors more quickly and more visibly, such a system may stimulate learning by doing in a way that modular systems do not. This is indeed the benefit that so-called Japanese-style manufacturing systems (including just-in-time inventory systems) are said to take advantage of: since the failure of any one part can cause total system breakdown, interdependency raises the cost of missing or poorly functioning parts, which in turn raises the incentive to make sure that each part is of high quality.

---

[3] The Wrights did control the lateral stability of the plane by twisting the wing, an idea they got from watching buzzards fly (Bittlingmayer 1988, pp. 230–232). Soon, however, others, including Alexander Graham Bell, further decoupled mechanical from biological design by introducing the concept of the aileron to control lateral stability.

Influenced by the success of highly modular systems in the computer sector, American automobile manufacturers in the 1990s attempted a strategy of modularity-plus-outsourcing (Jacobides, MacDuffie and Tae 2016). This was essentially the Hora approach: conceptualize the automobile as an arrangement of stable complex subsystems that could be outsourced to capable suppliers and then easily put together on assembly lines shorter and simpler than was traditional, effectively distributing complexity upstream (Alochet, MacDuffie and Midler 2023, pp. 64–65). But the industry quickly learned that this was a mistake. By assembling vehicles as more nearly unitary systems at final assembly, the car companies could retain control of the knowledge necessary to manufacture, and could better assure the quality of, a complex product that was in the end far less modular than the digital computer.[4] In effect, the automobile industry abandoned Hora for Tempus.

Following Kauffman (1993), many scholars have modeled adaptation to a given environment as a process of climbing hills in rugged terrain (so-called NK-models). If myopic agents cannot envision the terrain synoptically but know only whether they are ascending or descending, the optimizing agents may find themselves trapped on a small hill (a local optimum) instead of sitting on the highest of all peaks (the global optimum). Some have argued that a modular system is more likely to end up on a local optimum (Marengo and Dosi 2005), even though it may discover a pretty good hilltop ages before any non-modular alternative has slogged its way to Shangri-la. In any event, model results are highly sensitive to assumptions, and perhaps the most we can say is that a system faced with the problem of adapting to a given environment – a given optimization problem – is best served not by maximizing the modularity of its architecture but by finding the optimal degree of modularity (Frenken and Mendritzki 2012, p. 943).

Innovation that takes place through changes in the modules is called *modular innovation*. This is in contrast to what Henderson and Clark (1990) call *architectural innovation*, in which the parts change slowly but the architecture connecting them changes rapidly. Notice, however, that architectural innovation need not always imply a change in the system's

---

[4] It is a much-discussed topic in the literature of modularity whether the extent of modularity in the structure of production or organization must "mirror" the modular structure of the product being produced (Colfer and Baldwin 2016).

visible design rules: LEGO and Tinkertoys are classic modular systems designed for architectural innovation. Here, the architecture — the way the unchanging parts are recombined — can change, often in dramatic fashion, without any changes in the overall modularization (meaning the system interfaces and the way subsystems are partitioned into modules). A pile of LEGO bricks can even become a statue of Mark Twain.[5]

John Holland (2014) and other complexity theorists distinguish between *complex physical systems* and *complex adaptive systems*. In a similar vein, Carliss Baldwin (2019) distinguishes between *step processes* and *platforms*. Although there are many subtleties involved, the principal distinction is that complex physical systems (including step processes) are directed at a particular goal or function, like manufacturing an automobile, whereas complex adaptive systems (platform systems) create an open-ended framework of learning, interaction, and adaptation. A platform can be embodied in technology: an iPhone is an open-ended system for which people are constantly imagining new uses. Alternatively, however, a "platform" can be a disembodied system of rules – of institutions. Language is a good example. A language is a complex system in which words can be recombined (like LEGO) according to a shared set of rules in an essentially infinite variety of ways (Pinker 2000). Social conventions in general are platforms: a shared rule that everyone must drive on the right-hand side of the road reduces transaction costs and enables an infinite variety of trips, in much the same way that a language enables an infinite variety of messages.

Notice that it is the fixed and predictable character of modularization that spurs innovation. Sometimes, of course, improving the functioning of a system calls for remodularization rather than recombination. Since a remodularization will render the existing stock of modules incompatible or irrelevant, systemic innovation comes at a cost. This indeed is one of the central insights of the much-discussed literature on path dependency and technical standards.

---

[5] Which you can see at the Mark Twain House museum in Hartford, Connecticut. If you arrive via Bradley International Airport, you can also see a model of the Twain House itself in the airport lobby, along with a model of the Goodspeed Opera House.

Box 9.1 QWERTY

In 1984, the economic historian Paul David was invited to present a paper at a session of the annual meeting of the American Economic Association devoted to the relationship between economics and economic history. Not wanting merely to repeat platitudes, David resolved to demonstrate to the assembled economists – who included Nobel Laureate Kenneth Arrow and soon-to-be laureate Robert Solow – that history was not merely enriching and educational but actually crucial for doing economics. Economic outcomes in the present, he would demonstrate, sometimes could not be explained by factors operating in the present. Sometimes outcomes could be explained only by singular – and perhaps even random – events in the past. Very often, he argued, what we observe today depends on the path history took.

David's example would be the standard arrangement of keys on the English-language keyboards of typewriters and computers (David 1985). His presentation would mushroom into what is arguably the most widely known and discussed didactic fable in all of economics – perhaps in all of social science: the parable of QWERTY.

The late nineteenth century in the United States was a period of inventive ferment in mechanical devices. Many tinkerers were working on the idea of what was to become the typewriter, ultimately a mashup of the printing press and the piano. Among these was Christopher Latham Sholes, who patented a device he had created with the help of his friend Carlos Glidden in 1867. Sholes worked to perfect the device, and by 1873 the arms maker E. Remington & Sons had acquired the manufacturing rights. The Sholes-Glidden design was the origin of the QWERTY keyboard, so called because of the arrangement of letters on the top row. (David speculated, probably correctly, that the arrangement was chosen in part so that a salesman could quickly peck out the words "type writer" during a demonstration.)

As the demand for office machinery took off in the 1880s, the QWERTY design became the standard we still use today. Standardization emerged, and was necessary, because of the invention of touch typing. The touch method sped up typing dramatically, but it required the expensive acquisition of cognitive skills linked tightly to the layout of keys. Effectively, as David put it, the tacit knowledge of the typist was the "software" that ran on the hardware of the typewriter. Because the cost of switching keyboard layouts was high, would-be typists wanted to learn the layout most employers used, just as office managers wanted to buy machines that had attracted the largest number of touch typists. The result is that both typists and offices triangulated on a common design; and the larger the number of people who adopted the design, the more attractive the design became to others. This positive-feedback process David called "QWERTY-nomics."

Two claims made David's account particularly salient: (1) that the triumph of the Sholes-Glidden-Remington layout resulted not from its technical superiority but from a historical accident – thus affirming the importance of history – and (2) that the success of this design locked society into what was an inefficient standard. In 1932, August Dvorak, a proponent of scientific management (and a cousin of the famed composer), had patented an alternative layout that, David insisted, outperforms QWERTY because it groups more common letters on and near the home row and thus reduces the average distance the fingers must travel. Despite the self-evident superiority of the Dvorak design, David complained, we are stuck with QWERTY. Path dependency can lead, and in this case has led, to an inefficient outcome.

It is hard to overstate the enthusiasm with which the meme of QWERTY-nomics was received within economics and well beyond. Inevitably, of course, critics arose. The most important of these were Stanley Liebowitz and Stephen Margolis (1990). David had treated the early prominence of QWERTY as an unexplained random event; another account claimed that QWERTY got its all-important head start by winning a major typing contest in Cincinnati in 1888. Liebowitz and Margolis argued that there was, in fact, intense competition among alternatives – and many typing contests – at the time, suggesting that the Remington machine was succeeding because of technical superiority, not random chance. They also provided detailed evidence calling into question the superiority of the Dvorak keyboard. There is more to the ergonomics of keyboards than the travel time of fingers. Rhythm is important as – crucially – is the ability of the design to avoid the constant jamming of typebars when two keys are struck at nearly the same instant (a problem I well remember from my much-used Smith Corona portable). Neil Kay (2013) has argued not only that jamming was the crucial engineering problem, but that Sholes and his successors had actually devised and implemented in QWERTY a simple principle of key placement, which they went so far as to protect with intellectual property rights, that approximately minimized jamming. In Kay's computer simulations of jamming, QWERTY always beats Dvorak by a wide margin.

Arguably, the more important contribution of Liebowitz and Margolis (1995) is the framework they offered for thinking about problems of path dependency. In *first-degree path dependency*, today's outcome depends on events from the past, but there is no issue of inefficiency. We drive on the right (in the U.S.) for historical reasons, but we would not have been better off choosing the left. In *second-degree path dependency*, outcomes today depend on historical events, and today we may regret the path taken, but given the institutions and knowledge available at the time the path was chosen, no better choice could have been made. Only in the case of *third-degree path dependency* is there any inefficiency: not only is the path chosen regrettable today, but a better path could have been chosen in the past given what was known and possible in the past.

It is controversial whether history offers any examples of third-degree path dependency. If Kay is right, it's not even clear that QWERTY is an example of second-degree path dependency (Margolis 2013, pp. 1189–1190). For the near century between the introduction of the Remington typewriter and the introduction of the electronic IBM Selectric in 1961, QWERTY would have been preferable to a layout that minimized the movement of fingers. By the end of the twentieth century, the typing of information onto paper as a system of data storage had become obsolete, and typing speed effectively ceased to matter. If the choice of QWERTY as a standard was ever regrettable, it was only for two or three decades at most.

We are now in a position to make the connection between modular systems and the economics of organization.

For one thing, there is a natural fit between the theory of modular (nearly decomposable) systems and the theory of property rights we talked about in Chapter 5. Rights are about encapsulation and information hiding. As Hayek argued, a well-functioning social platform must "demarcate for every individual a range of permitted actions by designating … ranges of objects over which only particular individuals are allowed to dispose and from the control of which all others are excluded. The range of actions in which each will be secured against the interference of others can be determined by rules equally applicable to all only if these rules make it possible to ascertain which particular objects each may command for his purposes. In other words, rules are required which make it possible at each moment to ascertain the boundary of the protected domain of each and thus to distinguish between the *meum* and the *tuum*" (Hayek 1973, p. 107).

At the broadest level, the system of private property rights is a modular system of abstract rules – a platform – that permits individual agents to pursue an infinite variety of goals. It also permits the recombination of ideas that generate economic growth. As Hayek famously argued, price becomes an anonymous interface allowing billions of individual agents to specialize and trade with one another without having to communicate rich information (Hayek 1945).

Henry Smith (2012) has proposed that the logic of modular systems should underpin our understanding of the law of property. For the most part, he points out, the law relies on an exclusion strategy. Non-owners do not have to know any of the details of how or why a piece of property is owned or how that property is being used. They need only know that as non-owners, they are excluded from interfering with the use of the property unless they receive permission to do so.[6] This economizes dramatically on information and transaction costs. Property rights inhere in the thing owned: they are rights *in rem*. This stands in contrast to rights granted by contract, which are typically rights *in personam*, that is, rights that specify particular named individuals and thus call for the exchange of far more complex and detailed information.

As both Hayek and Smith are well aware, drawing module boundaries may not always be straightforward and may be difficult when there are externalities. Indeed, we can think of externalities precisely as failures of encapsulation. Thus, in many cases, Smith argues, the exclusion strategy of property law needs to be supplemented with a strategy of *governance*: the use of rules that are less general and more contextual than the abstract rules of ownership[7] (Smith 2002). Governance strategies call for more of the "knowledge of the particular circumstances of time and place" (Hayek 1945, p. 521).

As economists now understand, externalities are ultimately a manifestation of the character of things owned – of goods – themselves, and, as we

---

[6] As Sir William Blackstone famously put it, a right to property is "that sole and despotic dominion which one man claims and exercises over the external things of the world, in total exclusion of the right of any other individual in the universe" (Blackstone 1765, II.i.2).

[7] Think back here to our discussion in Chapter 5 of the property rule versus the liability rule as mechanisms for protecting entitlements (Calabresi and Melamed 1972). The liability rule is an example of a governance mechanism requiring considerable local contextual information.

have seen, thinking about the characteristics of goods is a more general framework for thinking about ownership boundaries. Not all goods are simple private goods, which are rival in use and also easily excludable in use. Some goods, for example, are what Elinor Ostrom (2015), following James Buchanan, called *club goods*: they are rivalrous in use – Ostrom preferred the term "subtractable" – but they do not lend themselves easily to the drawing of exclusion boundaries. Such goods thus frequently require governance strategies. Ostrom analyzed many such strategies in a multiplicity of situations in history and around the world. She found that in simple face-to-face societies – *within* modules, in effect – governance strategies work well in allocating resources. The information demands of small societies are low, and thus so are the costs of using information-intensive approaches and of tailoring rules to specific individuals and specific contexts.[8]

Throughout the book, but especially in Chapter 6, we made what was, in essence, a tripartite distinction among markets, complex (often relational) contracts, and internal organization. Now we can understand these alternatives more clearly in the framework of modularity.

In the language of Carliss Baldwin (2008), transactions are the movement of materials, energy, and information between tasks.[9] Markets constitute *thin crossing points* at which transactions can take place with low information costs, just as Hayek argued. For a transfer to take place at a thin crossing point, it must be *defined, counted,* and *compensated.* For transfers at thin crossing points, simple exclusion strategies, meaning property rights and property rules, work well. But the process of defining, counting, and compensating requires social institutions, not just for the counting and compensating – which may imply, for example, some

---

8   Ostrom also found that in more complex property situations, systems of rules often evolve spontaneously. This is true even of rules that are more abstract than the highly contextual rules of small face-to-face groups, albeit less abstract than the first-order rules of the law of property. Very often these rules involve multiple centers of authority over exclusion and use, what Ostrom called *polycentricity.* This too is a form of modularity.

9   Baldwin wants to restrict the term "transaction" to those transfers that can be defined, counted, and compensated – that is, to market transfers (so did Harold Demsetz [1988, pp. 144–145]). In keeping with what is probably more typical (if perhaps sloppier) usage, I will continue to call transfers "transactions" even if they occur within firms or across complex or relational contracts.

kind of monetary system, however rudimentary – but even for the defining, which requires the social institution of standardization.

Box 9.2 The grain elevator

In the American Midwest before the coming of the railroad, as indeed throughout much of agricultural history, wheat was stored, shipped, and traded by the sack. Each sack of wheat was the product of a specific identifiable farmer, which meant that repeated trades could generate reputation effects that assured the quality of the grain in the market. At the same time, however, this mode of storage meant large transaction costs: the transportation costs of shipping the sacks by wagon and river to St. Louis or Chicago; brokerage fees; insurance premiums; the implicit costs of price volatility and poor information about market prices at the destination; and the cost of the stevedores lugging bags from warehouse to barge to warehouse. According to one (clearly exaggerated) contemporary account, a "10,000-bushel shipment of grain arriving in St. Louis might involve 'the labor of probably two or three hundred Irishmen, negroes and mules for a couple of days'" (Cronon 1991, p. 112). Even the burlap bags themselves cost two to four cents apiece. The principal transaction costs in this system were thus arguably incurred on a per-sack basis as part of the process of exchanging title to the wheat. It was as if some – perhaps most – of the grain spilled out of the sack between farmer and miller.

All of this changed with the coming of the railroad in the mid-nineteenth century. It quickly became economical to store and ship wheat in bulk, using the newly invented mechanical grain elevator. A typical large elevator of the era could simultaneously empty twelve railroad cars and load two ships at the rate of 24,000 bushels per hour. But, as elevators necessitated mixing together the grain of many different farmers, the new technology destroyed the old system of quality control that had relied on reputational effects from repeated transactions with identifiable farmers. Farmers could now cheat by mixing in inferior grain. To solve this problem, the Chicago Mercantile Exchange paid the costs of creating standardized categories for wheat and persuading farmers and buyers to adopt those standards. In addition, they needed to cover the costs of inspecting the wheat for conformance to the standards, which they did by commissioning inspectors.

Like the case of telephone switching, this example demonstrates that mechanization typically demands a thoroughgoing redesign of the architecture of production tasks. But it also sheds light on the concept of transaction costs. In the days of burlap sacks, transaction costs were mostly what Carliss Baldwin (2008) calls *mundane* transaction costs. We can think of them as frictions in the task-and-transfer system. But as we have seen in most of the middle chapters of this book, the economics of organization is concerned prominently with other kinds of transaction costs, notably those arising from moral hazard and opportunism of one sort or another. The example of the grain elevator shows that there are trade-offs between mundane transaction costs and the transaction costs of opportunism – and, perhaps more significantly, trade-offs between production costs and transaction costs. The grain elevator (along with the railroad) dramatically reduced both mundane transaction costs and the production costs of grain distribution. It did this at the expense of increasing opportunism transaction costs, even if these were in the end small in comparison and could be dealt with cheaply. Note also that the grain-elevator system substituted fixed costs for per-unit costs: not just the fixed costs of the machinery but also the fixed (not per-unit) costs of creating standards and maintaining the modularization. These too are a form of transaction costs. They are the costs of running the economic system (Allen 2000; Langlois 2006).

In many cases, as we have seen, it may not be worth the cost to define, count, and compensate what is transferred (like salt in a restaurant). More significantly, it may not make sense to simplify and standardize transactions. In an uncertain and changing world, knowledge structures are in flux, and rich information often needs to be transferred between tasks. Even in the simple case of the parable of the secretary, where transactions could, in principle, have been defined, it would have been expensive or impossible to count and compensate them individually. The same was true, albeit for slightly different reasons, in the Alchian and Demsetz story of team production. In both cases, it made more sense to govern the transactions within a firm.

And this, of course, is the point. We can think of firms as modules in which rich, complex information can be transferred between tasks more cheaply and fluidly than via market transactions. Baldwin (2008, p. 183) calls this *transactional encapsulation*. She illustrates this idea with what we can call the parable of the pot hook. A kitchen of significant size requires a division of tasks to produce meals: a chef, sous-chefs, dishwashers, and all the rest. But it also requires kitchen implements. If we imagine production taking place in olden (maybe medieval) times, those implements – like a pot hook, for example – would also be produced with a relatively simple set of tasks. We can understand the task structure of the whole process – making the implements and cooking the food – using the matrix formulation introduced in Figure 9.1. (See Figure 9.2.)

There would need to be some minimal informational exchange between the kitchen and the smithy, but that would be limited to basic understandings of what a pot hook is and what it does. This is indicated by column a_1, here labeled CG for "common ground." For the most part, however, there would be little transfer of materials, energy, and information between the kitchen and the smithy. Dense transfers would take place *within* what are separate modules. The two modules would be connected only by a thin crossing point, at which the finished pot hook – defined, counted, and compensated – would be sold by the smithy and bought by the kitchen. Notice that this representation also speaks to our concept of *capabilities*: it shows graphically why it makes little sense for the smithy to try to cook its own food, and no sense at all for the kitchen to try to make its own metal tools.

Figure 9.2 depicts a de facto grouping of tasks into modules or "firms." But modularity also arguably lies behind formal legal rules as well. Just as property law is the law of modular things, corporate law can be seen as

		CG	S1	S2	S3	S4	S5	K1	K2	K3	K4	K5
			Smithy					Kitchen				
	CG	.										
Smithy	S1	X	.	X	X	X	X					
	S2	X	X	.	X	X	X					
	S3	X	X	X	.	X	X					
	S4	X	X	X	X	.	X					
	S5	X	X	X	X	X	.					
Kitchen	K1	X	Pot Hook			X	→	.	X	X	X	X
	K2	X	Transfer					X	.	X	X	X
	K3	X						X	X	.	X	X
	K4	X						X	X	X	.	X
	K5	X						X	X	X	X	.

Source: Baldwin (2008), used by permission of Oxford University Press.

Figure 9.2   Task matrix of the smithy and the kitchen

the law of modular legal *entities*, in effect a higher-level modularization (Smith 2012, pp. 1722–1723). We saw in Chapter 6 that corporate law partitions assets into a private sphere and a corporate sphere, effectively insulating the assets of the corporation from the claims of the creditors of the owners (Hansmann and Kraakman 2000). The corporation is modular in other ways as well. The institution of alienable shares allows suppliers of capital to enter and exit easily by trading pieces of ownership at thin crossing points. Owners of corporate shares can themselves be corporations, taking advantage of the "nesting" property of modular systems to create the pyramidal holding company form of corporate governance that dominates most of the world (Kandel, Kosenko, Morck and Yafeh 2015). In the U.S., which actively discouraged the holding company for much of the twentieth century, the multidivisional (or M-form) structure arose to modularize corporations into wholly owned divisions instead of publicly traded subsidiaries (Chandler 1962).

As in the Coasean economics of organization, in the modular approach, the market (trading at thin crossing points) and the firm (fully encapsulated modules) are not the only alternatives. It may often make sense to trade at thick crossing points. In some cases, this means relational contracts, which develop over time and in which not all transfers are explicitly defined, counted, and compensated. It may also mean some of the other forms of complex contracts – and hybrid forms – we have examined. Indeed, most examples of complex contracting partake of modularity in that they operate through the partitioning of rights and the enforcement of exclusion. Franchising, for example, is a partitioning of ownership between local operators (with high-powered incentives) and the proprietors of brand name capital and other fixed assets (with economies of scale).

Suggested readings

Carliss Y. Baldwin, "Where Do Transactions Come From? Modularity, Transactions, and the Boundaries of Firms," *Industrial and Corporate Change* **17**(1): 155–195, February 2008.

Richard N. Langlois, "Modularity in Technology and Organization," *Journal of Economic Behavior & Organization* **49**(1): 19–37, September 2002.

Herbert A. Simon, "The Architecture of Complexity," *Proceedings of the American Philosophical Society* **106**(6): 467–482, 1962.

Henry E. Smith, "Property as the Law of Things," *Harvard Law Review* **125**(7): 1691–1726, 2012.

References

Acemoglu, Daron. 2003. "Why Not a Political Coase Theorem? Social Conflict, Commitment, and Politics," *Journal of Comparative Economics* **31**(4): 620–652.

Acemoglu, Daron, and David Autor. 2012. "What Does Human Capital Do? A Review of Goldin and Katz's 'the Race between Education and Technology,'" *Journal of Economic Literature* **50**(2): 426–463.

Agrawal, Ajay, Joshua Gans and Avi Goldfarb. 2018. *Prediction Machines: The Simple Economics of Artificial Intelligence.* Boston: Harvard Business Review Press.

Agarwal, Nikhil, Alex Moehring, Pranav Rajpurkar and Tobias Salz. 2023. "Combining Human Expertise with Artificial Intelligence: Experimental Evidence from Radiology," National Bureau of Economic Research Working Paper Series No. 31422.

Aitken, Hugh G. J. 1985. *The Continuous Wave: Technology and American Radio, 1900–1932.* Princeton, NJ: Princeton University Press.

Alchian, Armen. 1959. "Costs and Output," in Paul Baran, Tibor Scitovsky and Edward S. Shaw, eds., *The Allocation of Economic Resources.* Stanford: Stanford University Press, pp. 23–40.

Alchian, Armen A. 1950. "Uncertainty, Evolution, and Economic Theory," *The Journal of Political Economy* **58**(3): 211–221.

Alchian, Armen A., and Harold Demsetz. 1972. "Production, Information Costs, and Economic Organization," *American Economic Review* **62**(5): 772–795.

Alchian, Armen A., and Susan Woodward. 1988. "The Firm Is Dead; Long Live the Firm: A Review of Oliver E. Williamson's *The Economic Institutions of Capitalism*," *Journal of Economic Literature* **26**(1): 65–79.

Allen, Douglas W. 2000. "Transaction Costs," in Boudewijn Bouckaert and Gerrit De Geest, eds., *The Encyclopedia of Law and Economics.* Cheltenham: Edward Elgar, pp. 893–926.

Allen, Douglas W., and Yoram Barzel. 2016. "Coase's Contribution to Contract Theory," in Claude Ménard and Elodie Bertrand, eds., *The Elgar Companion to Ronald H. Coase.* Cheltenham: Edward Elgar, pp. 68–82.

Allen, Douglas W., and Dean Lueck. 2004. *The Nature of the Farm: Contracts, Risk, and Organization in Agriculture.* Cambridge, MA: The MIT Press.

Allen, G. C. 1929. *The Industrial Development of Birmingham and the Black Country, 1906–1927.* London: Allen & Unwin.

Alochet, Marc, John Paul MacDuffie and Christophe Midler. 2023. "Mirroring in Production? Early Evidence from the Scale-up of Battery Electric Vehicles (BEVs)," *Industrial and Corporate Change* **32**(1): 61–111.

Altbach, Philip G., Edward Choi, Mathew R. Allen and Hans de Wit. 2019. *The Global Phenomenon of Family-Owned or Managed Universities*. Leiden: Brill.

Ames, Edward, and Nathan Rosenberg. 1965. "The Progressive Division and Specialization of Industries," *The Journal of Development Studies* **1**(4): 363–383.

Autor, David H. 2013. "The 'Task Approach' to Labor Markets: An Overview," *Journal for Labour Market Research* **46**(3): 185–199.

Autor, David H. 2014. "Polanyi's Paradox and the Shape of Employment Growth," *National Bureau of Economic Research Working Paper* Series No. 20485.

Autor, David H. 2024. "Applying AI to Rebuild Middle Class Jobs," *National Bureau of Economic Research Working Paper* Series No. 32140.

Autor, David H., Frank Levy and Richard J. Murnane. 2003. "The Skill Content of Recent Technological Change: An Empirical Exploration," *The Quarterly Journal of Economics* **118**(4): 1279–1333 (November 1).

Babbage, Charles. 1846. *On the Economy of Machinery and Manufactures*. London: John Murray.

Baldwin, Carliss Y. 2008. "Where Do Transactions Come From? Modularity, Transactions, and the Boundaries of Firms," *Industrial and Corporate Change* **17**(1): 155–195 (February).

Baldwin, Carliss Y. 2019. "Platform Systems vs. Step Processes—the Value of Options and the Power of Modularity," *Harvard Business School Working Paper* No. 19–073 (January).

Baldwin, Carliss Y., and Kim B. Clark. 2000. *Design Rules: The Power of Modularity*. Cambridge, MA: The MIT Press.

Barzel, Yoram. 1982. "Measurement Cost and the Organization of Markets," *Journal of Law and Economics* **25**(1): 27–48.

Barzel, Yoram. 1987. "The Entrepreneur's Reward for Self-Policing," *Economic Inquiry* **25**(1): 103–116.

Barzel, Yoram. 1997. *Economic Analysis of Property Rights*. New York: Cambridge University Press, second edition.

Barzel, Yoram, and Douglas W. Allen. 2023. *Economic Analysis of Property Rights*. New York: Cambridge University Press, third edition.

Baum, Nancy. 2010. "Physician Ownership in Hospitals and Outpatient Facilities," Ann Arbor: Center for Healthcare Research and Transformation.

Berle, Adolf A., and Gardiner C. Means. 1930. "Corporations and the Public Investor," *The American Economic Review* **20**(1): 54–71.

Berle, Adolf A., and Gardiner C. Means. 1932. *The Modern Corporation and Private Property*. New York: Macmillan.

Bhattacharyya, Sugato, and Francine Lafontaine. 1995. "Double-Sided Moral Hazard and the Nature of Share Contracts," *The RAND Journal of Economics* **26**(4): 761–781.

Bittlingmayer, George. 1988. "Property Rights, Progress, and the Aircraft Patent Agreement," *The Journal of Law & Economics* **31**(1): 227–248.

Blackstone, William. 1765. *Commentaries on the Laws of England.* Oxford: Clarendon Press.

Blair, Margaret M. 2003. "Locking in Capital: What Corporate Law Achieved for Business Organizers in the Nineteenth Century," *UCLA Law Review* **51**: 387–455 (December).

Blair, Roger D. and Francine Lafontaine. 2006. "Understanding the Economics of Franchising and the Laws That Regulate It," *Franchise Law Journal* **26**(2): 55–66.

Bolton, Patrick, and David S. Scharfstein. 2000. "Response from Patrick Bolton and David S. Scharfstein," *The Journal of Economic Perspectives* **14**(2): 234–236.

Bowman, Ward S., Jr. 1957. "Tying Arrangements and the Leverage Problem," *The Yale Law Journal* **67**(1): 19–37.

Brandeis, Louis D. 1913. "Cutthroat Prices: The Competition That Kills," *Harper's Weekly* **58**: 10–12.

Breit, William. 1991. "Resale Price Maintenance: What Do Economists Know and When Did They Know It?" *Journal of Institutional and Theoretical Economics* **147**(1): 72–90.

Brooks, Fred. 1975. *The Mythical Man-Month.* New York: Addison-Wesley.

Brooks, Richard R. W. 2016. "The Holdup Game," in Claude Ménard and Elodie Bertrand, eds., *The Elgar Companion to Ronald H. Coase.* Cheltenham: Edward Elgar, pp. 131–147.

Brynjolfsson, Erik, and Andrew McAfee. 2014. *The Second Machine Age: Work, Progress, and Prosperity in a Time of Brilliant Technologies.* New York: W. W. Norton.

Buchanan, James M. 1990. "The Domain of Constitutional Economics," *Constitutional Political Economy* **1**(1): 1–18.

Buchanan, James M., and Yong J. Yoon. 2000. "Symmetric Tragedies: Commons and Anticommons," *The Journal of Law and Economics* **43**(1): 1–13.

Calabresi, Guido, and A. Douglas Melamed. 1972. "Property Rules, Liability Rules, and Inalienability: One View of the Cathedral," *Harvard Law Review* **85**(6): 1089–1128.

Cameron, Rondo E., and Larry Neal. 2003. *A Concise Economic History of the World: From Paleolithic Times to the Present.* New York: Oxford University Press, Fourth Edition.

Carlos, Ann M., and Frank D. Lewis. 2010. *Commerce by a Frozen Sea: Native Americans and the European Fur Trade.* Philadelphia: University of Pennsylvania Press.

Chandler, Alfred D., Jr. 1962. *Strategy and Structure: Chapters in the History of the Industrial Enterprise.* Cambridge, MA: MIT Press.

Chandler, Alfred D., Jr. 1977. *The Visible Hand: The Managerial Revolution in American Business.* Cambridge, MA: Belknap Press.

Chandler, Alfred D., Jr., and Stephen Salsbury. 1971. *Pierre S. Du Pont and the Making of the Modern Corporation.* New York: Harper & Row.

Chetham, Deirdre. 2002. *Before the Deluge: The Vanishing World of the Yangtze's Three Gorges.* New York: Palgrave Macmillan.

Cheung, Steven N. S. 1983. "The Contractual Nature of the Firm," *Journal of Law and Economics* **26**(1): 1–21 (April).

Cheung, Steven N. S. 2018. "Theory of Share Tenancy after 50 Years," *Man and the Economy* **5**(1): 2018-0006. https://doi.org/10.1515/me-2018-0006.

Christensen, Clayton M., Matt Verlinden and George Westerman. 2002. "Disruption, Disintegration and the Dissipation of Differentiability," *Industrial and Corporate Change* **11**(5): 955–993 (November).

Coase, Ronald H. 1937. "The Nature of the Firm," *Economica* (N.S.) **4**: 386–405.

Coase, Ronald H. 1960. "The Problem of Social Cost," *The Journal of Law and Economics* **3**: 1–44.

Coase, Ronald H. 1972. "Industrial Organization: A Proposal for Research," in Victor R. Fuchs, ed., *Economic Research: Retrospect and Prospect, Volume 3, Policy Issues and Research Opportunities in Industrial Organization*. New York: Columbia University Press for the National Bureau of Economic Research, pp. 59–73.

Coase, Ronald H. 1988a. *The Firm, the Market, and the Law*. Chicago: University of Chicago Press.

Coase, Ronald H. 1988b. "The Nature of the Firm: Influence," *Journal of Law, Economics and Organization* **4**(1): 33–47.

Coase, Ronald H. 1988c. "The Nature of the Firm: Origin," *Journal of Law, Economics and Organization* **4**(1): 3–17.

Coase, Ronald H. 2006. "The Conduct of Economics: The Example of Fisher Body and General Motors," *Journal of Economics and Management Strategy* **15**(2): 255–78.

Cohen, Ben. 2023. "These People Are Responsible for the Cranberry Sauce You Love to Hate," *The Wall Street Journal*, November 17. https://www.wsj.com/business/ocean-spray-cranberries-cooperative-thanksgiving-c57febfc.

Colfer, Lyra J., and Carliss Y. Baldwin. 2016. "The Mirroring Hypothesis: Theory, Evidence, and Exceptions," *Industrial and Corporate Change* **25**(5): 709–738 (October).

Cronon, William. 1983. *Changes in the Land: Indians, Colonists, and the Ecology of New England*. New York: Hill and Wang.

Cronon, William. 1991. *Nature's Metropolis: Chicago and the Great West*. New York: W. W. Norton.

Cyert, Richard M., and James G. March. 1963. *A Behavioral Theory of the Firm*. Englewood Cliffs, NJ: Prentice-Hall.

David, Paul A. 1985. "Clio and the Economics of QWERTY," *The American Economic Review* **75**(2): 332–337.

Demsetz, Harold. 1967. "Toward a Theory of Property Rights," *The American Economic Review* **57**(2): 347–359.

Demsetz, Harold. 1969. "Information and Efficiency: Another Viewpoint," *Journal of Law and Economics* **12**(1): 1–22.

Demsetz, Harold. 1988. "The Theory of the Firm Revisited," *Journal of Law, Economics and Organization* **4**(1): 141–161.

Director, Aaron, and Edward H. Levi. 1956. "Law and the Future: Trade Regulation," *Northwestern University Law Review* **51**(2): 281–296.

Drucker, Peter F. 1976. *The Unseen Revolution: How Pension Fund Socialism Came to America*. New York: Harper & Row.

Farnie, Douglas A. 1979. *The English Cotton Industry and the World Market, 1815–1896*. Oxford: Clarendon Press.

Fehr, Ernst, and Simon Gächter. 2000. "Fairness and Retaliation: The Economics of Reciprocity," *Journal of Economic Perspectives* **14**(3): 159–181.

Feigenbaum, James, and Daniel P. Gross. 2024a. "Answering the Call of Automation: How the Labor Market Adjusted to the Mechanization of Telephone Operation," *The Quarterly Journal of Economics* **139**(3): 1879–1939.

Feigenbaum, James, and Daniel P. Gross. 2024b. "Organizational and Economic Obstacles to Automation: A Cautionary Tale from AT&T in the Twentieth Century," *Management Science*, published online, accessed 05.11.24: https://doi.org/10.1287/mnsc.2022.01760.

Fisher, Franklin M., James W. McKie and Richard B. Mancke. 1983. *IBM and the U. S. Data Processing Industry*. New York: Praeger.

Foss, Kirsten, and Nicolai J. Foss. 2001. "Assets, Attributes and Ownership," *International Journal of the Economics of Business* **8**(1): 19–37.

Freeland, Robert F. 2000. "Creating Holdup through Vertical Integration: Fisher Body Revisited," *Journal of Law and Economics* **43**(1): 33–66.

Frenken, Koen, and Stefan Mendritzki. 2012. "Optimal Modularity: A Demonstration of the Evolutionary Advantage of Modular Architectures," *Journal of Evolutionary Economics* **22**(5): 935–956.

Friedman, Milton. 1953. "The Methodology of Positive Economics," in *Essays in Positive Economics*. Chicago: University of Chicago Press, pp. 3–43.

Friedman, Milton. 1970. "The Social Responsibility of Business Is to Increase Its Profits," *The New York Times Magazine*, September 13, p. 32–3.

Gibbons, Robert. 2005. "Four Formal(izable) Theories of the Firm?" *Journal of Economic Behavior & Organization* **58**(2): 200–245.

Gibbons, Robert, and Rebecca Henderson. 2012. "Relational Contracts and Organizational Capabilities," *Organization Science* **23**(5): 1350–1364.

Gould, Stephen Jay. 1983. *Hen's Teeth and Horse's Toes*. New York: W. W. Norton.

Graham, Margaret B. W. 1986. *RCA and the Videodisk: The Business of Research*. New York: Cambridge University Press.

Grattan-Guinness, Ivor. 1990. "Work for the Hairdressers: The Production of De Prony's Logarithmic and Trigonometric Tables," *IEEE Annals of the History of Computing* **12**(3): 177–185.

Greif, Avner. 2006. "Family Structure, Institutions, and Growth: The Origins and Implications of Western Corporations," *The American Economic Review* **96**(2): 308–312.

Grossman, Sanford J., and Oliver D. Hart. 1986. "The Costs and Benefits of Ownership: A Theory of Vertical and Lateral Integration," *The Journal of Political Economy* **94**(4): 691–719.

Halberstam, David. 1986. *The Reckoning*. New York: William Morrow & Co.

Hansmann, Henry. 1988. "Ownership of the Firm," *Journal of Law, Economics and Organization* **4**(2): 267–304.

Hansmann, Henry. 1996. *The Ownership of Enterprise*. Cambridge, MA: Belknap Press.

Hansmann, Henry. 2014. "All Firms Are Cooperatives – and So Are Governments," *Journal of Entrepreneurial and Organizational Diversity* 2(2): 1–10 (January).

Hansmann, Henry, and Reinier Kraakman. 2000. "Organization Law as Asset Partitioning," *European Economic Review* 44(4–6): 807–817.

Hart, Oliver D. 1988. "Incomplete Contracts and the Theory of the Firm," *Journal of Law, Economics and Organization* 4(1): 119–139.

Hart, Oliver D. 1989. "An Economist's Perspective on the Theory of the Firm," *Columbia Law Review* 89(7): 1757–1774.

Hart, Oliver D., and John Moore. 1990. "Property Rights and the Nature of the Firm," *The Journal of Political Economy* 98(6): 1119–1158.

Hawes, Colin. 2021. "Why Is Huawei's Ownership So Strange? A Case Study of the Chinese Corporate and Socio-Political Ecosystem," *Journal of Corporate Law Studies* 21(1): 1–38.

Hayek, F. A. 1945. "The Use of Knowledge in Society," *The American Economic Review* 35(4): 519–530.

Hayek, F. A. 1973. *Law, Legislation, and Liberty. Volume 1: Rules and Order*. Chicago: University of Chicago Press.

Heller, Michael A. 1998. "The Tragedy of the Anticommons: Property in the Transition from Marx to Markets," *Harvard Law Review* 111(3): 621–688.

Heller, Michael A., and Rebecca S. Eisenberg. 1998. "Can Patents Deter Innovation? The Anticommons in Biomedical Research," *Science* 280: 698–701.

Henderson, Rebecca M., and Kim B. Clark. 1990. "Architectural Innovation: The Reconfiguration of Existing Product Technologies and the Failure of Established Firms," *Administrative Science Quarterly* 35(1): 9–30.

Hersey, John. 1956. *A Single Pebble*. New York: Alfred A. Knopf.

Hodgson, Geoffrey M. 2002. "The Legal Nature of the Firm and the Myth of the Firm-Market Hybrid," *International Journal of the Economics of Business* 9(1): 37–60.

Hodgson, Geoffrey M. 2023. "How Stable Routines Can Empower Varied Behaviors: Defining Routines as Organizational Capacities," *Industrial and Corporate Change* 32(6): 1319–1332.

Holcombe, Randall G. 2016. *Advanced Introduction to Public Choice*. Cheltenham: Edward Elgar.

Holland, John H. 2012. *Signals and Boundaries: Building Blocks for Complex Adaptive Systems*. Cambridge, MA: The MIT Press.

Holland, John H. 2014. *Complexity: A Very Short Introduction*. Oxford: Oxford University Press.

Holmström, Bengt, and Paul Milgrom. 1991. "Multitask Principal-Agent Analyses: Incentive Contracts, Asset Ownership, and Job Design," *Journal of Law, Economics, & Organization* 7(2): 24–52.

Holmström, Bengt, and Paul Milgrom. 1994. "The Firm as an Incentive System," *The American Economic Review* 84(4): 972–991.

Hounshell, David A. 1984. *From the American System to Mass Production, 1800–1932*. Baltimore: Johns Hopkins University Press.

Hovenkamp, Herbert. 2005. *The Antitrust Enterprise*. Cambridge, MA: Harvard University Press.

Howes, Anton. 2017. "The Spread of Improvement: Why Innovation Accelerated in Britain 1547–1851," Working Paper, Brown University. https://www .antonhowes.com/uploads/2/1/0/8/21082490/spread_of_improvement_ working_paper.pdf.

Jacobides, Michael G., John Paul MacDuffie and C. Jennifer Tae. 2016. "Agency, Structure, and the Dominance of OEMs: Change and Stability in the Automotive Sector," *Strategic Management Journal* **37**(9): 1942–1967.

Jensen, Michael C., and William H. Meckling. 1976. "Theory of the Firm: Managerial Behavior, Agency Costs and Ownership Structure," *Journal of Financial Economics* **3**(4): 305–360.

Jensen, Michael C., and William H. Meckling. 1992. "Specific and General Knowledge, and Organizational Structure," in Lars Werin and Hans Wijkander, eds., *Contract Economics*. Oxford: Basil Blackwell, pp. 251–74.

John, Richard R. 2010. *Network Nation: Inventing American Telecommunications*. Cambridge, MA: Harvard University Press.

Kandel, Eugene, Konstantin Kosenko, Randall Morck and Yishay Yafeh. 2015. "Business Groups in the United States: A Revised History of Corporate Ownership, Pyramids and Regulation, 1930–1950," *National Bureau of Economic Research Working Paper* No. 19691.

Kane, Carol K. 2021. "Recent Changes in Physician Practice Arrangements: Private Practice Dropped to Less Than 50 Percent of Physicians in 2020," Chicago: American Medical Association.

Katznelson, Ron D., and John Howells. 2014. "The Myth of the Early Aviation Patent Hold-up — How a U.S. Government Monopsony Commandeered Pioneer Airplane Patents," *Industrial and Corporate Change* **24**(1): 1–64.

Kauffman, Stuart A. 1993. *The Origins of Order. Self-Organization and Selection in Evolution*. New York: Oxford University Press.

Kay, Neil M. 2013. "Rerun the Tape of History and QWERTY Always Wins," *Research Policy* **42**(6–7): 1175–1185.

Kerr, Steven. 1975. "On the Folly of Rewarding A, while Hoping for B," *Academy of Management Journal* **18**(4): 769–783.

Kimball, Dexter S. 1929. *Industrial Economics*. New York: McGraw-Hill.

Kipling, Rudyard. 1902. *Just So Stories*. London: Macmillan.

KIPPRA. 2022. *The Establishment of the Kenya Institute for Public Policy Research and Analysis*. Nairobi: Kenya Institute for Public Policy Research and Analysis.

Klein, Benjamin. 1988. "Vertical Integration as Organizational Ownership: The Fisher Body-General Motors Relationship Revisited," *Journal of Law, Economics and Organization* **4**(1): 199–213.

Klein, Benjamin. 1996. "Why Hold-Ups Occur: The Self-Enforcing Range of Contractual Relationships," *Economic Inquiry* **34**(3): 444–463.

Klein, Benjamin, Robert G. Crawford and Armen A. Alchian. 1978. "Vertical Integration, Appropriable Rents, and the Competitive Contracting Process," *Journal of Law and Economics* **21**(2): 297–326.

Klein, Benjamin, and Keith B. Leffler. 1981. "The Role of Market Forces in Assuring Contractual Performance," *The Journal of Political Economy* **89**(4): 615–641.

Klein, Benjamin, and Kevin M. Murphy. 1988. "Vertical Restraints as Contract Enforcement Mechanisms," *The Journal of Law and Economics* **31**(2): 265–297.

Klepper, Steven. 2016. *Experimental Capitalism: The Nanoeconomics of American High-Tech Industries*. Princeton: Princeton University Press.

Knight, Frank H. 1921. *Risk, Uncertainty, and Profit*. Boston: Houghton-Mifflin.

Langlois, Richard N. 1984. "Internal Organization in a Dynamic Context: Some Theoretical Considerations," in Meheroo Jussawalla and Helene Ebenfield, eds., *Communication and Information Economics: New Perspectives*. Amsterdam: North-Holland, pp. 23–49.

Langlois, Richard N. 1986. "Rationality, Institutions, and Explanation," in Richard N. Langlois, ed., *Economics as a Process: Essays in the New Institutional Economics*. New York: Cambridge University Press, pp. 225–255.

Langlois, Richard N. 1990. "Bounded Rationality and Behavioralism: A Clarification and Critique," *Journal of Institutional and Theoretical Economics* **146**(4): 691–695 (December).

Langlois, Richard N. 1992. "Transaction Cost Economics in Real Time," *Industrial and Corporate Change* **1**(1): 99–127.

Langlois, Richard N. 1999. "Scale, Scope, and the Reuse of Knowledge," in Sheila C. Dow and Peter E. Earl, eds., *Economic Organization and Economic Knowledge: Essays in Honour of Brian J. Loasby*. Cheltenham: Edward Elgar, pp. 239–254.

Langlois, Richard N. 2003. "The Vanishing Hand: The Changing Dynamics of Industrial Capitalism," *Industrial and Corporate Change* **12**(2): 351–385 (April).

Langlois, Richard N. 2006. "The Secret Life of Mundane Transaction Costs," *Organization Studies* **27**(9): 1389–1410.

Langlois, Richard N. 2017. "The Institutional Approach to Economic History: Connecting the Two Strands," *Journal of Comparative Economics* **45**(1): 201–212 (February).

Langlois, Richard N. 2019. "The Corporation Is Not a Nexus of Contracts. It's an iPhone," in Francesca Gagliardi and David Gindis, eds., *Institutions and Evolution of Capitalism: Essays in Honour of Geoffrey M. Hodgson*. Cheltenham: Edward Elgar, pp. 142–156.

Langlois, Richard N. 2023. *The Corporation and the Twentieth Century: The History of American Business Enterprise*. Princeton, NJ: Princeton University Press.

Langlois, Richard N., and Pierre Garrouste. 1997. "Cognition, Redundancy, and Learning in Organizations," *Economics of Innovation and New Technology* **4**(4): 287–300.

Langlois, Richard N., and Giampaolo Garzarelli. 2008. "Of Hackers and Hairdressers: Modularity and the Organizational Economics of Open-Source Collaboration," *Industry & Innovation* **15**(2): 125–143 (April).

Langlois, Richard N., and Paul L. Robertson. 1989. "Explaining Vertical Integration: Lessons from the American Automobile Industry," *The Journal of Economic History* **49**(2): 361–375.

Langlois, Richard N., and Paul L. Robertson. 1992. "Networks and Innovation in a Modular System: Lessons from the Microcomputer and Stereo Component Industries," *Research Policy* **21**(4): 297–313.

Lavoie, Don C. 1985. *Rivalry and Central Planning.* New York: Cambridge University Press.

Lazarus, Barry A. 1991. "The Practice of Medicine and Prejudice in a New England Town: The Founding of Mount Sinai Hospital, Hartford, Connecticut," *Journal of American Ethnic History* **10**(3): 21–41.

Leijonhufvud, Axel. 1986. "Capitalism and the Factory System," in Richard N. Langlois, ed., *Economics as a Process: Essays in the New Institutional Economics.* New York: Cambridge University Press, pp. 203–223.

Lenin, Vladimir Ilyich. 1992 [1917]. *The State and Revolution.* London: Penguin.

Levitt, Steven D., John A. List and Chad Syverson. 2013. "Toward an Understanding of Learning by Doing: Evidence from an Automobile Assembly Plant," *Journal of Political Economy* **121**(4): 643–681.

Libecap, Gary D. 1984. "The Political Allocation of Mineral Rights: A Re-Evaluation of Teapot," *The Journal of Economic History* **44**(2): 381–391.

Libecap, Gary D. and Steven N. Wiggins. 1984. "Contractual Responses to the Common Pool: Prorationing of Crude Oil Production," *The American Economic Review* **74**(1): 87–98.

Liebowitz, S. J., and Stephen E. Margolis. 1990. "The Fable of the Keys," *Journal of Law and Economics* **33**(1): 1–25.

Liebowitz, S. J., and Stephen E. Margolis. 1995. "Path Dependence, Lock-in, and History," *Journal of Law, Economics, & Organization* **11**(1): 205–226.

Lipartito, Kenneth. 1994. "When Women Were Switches: Technology, Work, and Gender in the Telephone Industry, 1890–1920," *The American Historical Review* **99**(4): 1075–1111.

Lipartito, Kenneth, and Yumiko Morii. 2010. "Rethinking the Separation of Ownership from Management in American History," *University of Seattle Law Review* **33**(4): 1025–1063 (Summer).

Loasby, Brian J. 1976. *Choice, Complexity, and Ignorance.* Cambridge: Cambridge University Press.

Loasby, Brian J. 1991. *Equilibrium and Evolution: An Exploration of Connecting Principles in Economics.* Manchester: Manchester University Press.

Loasby, Brian J. 2002. "The Significance of Penrose's Theory for the Development of Economics," in Christos Pitelis, ed., *The Growth of the Firm: The Legacy of Edith Penrose.* Oxford: Oxford University Press, pp. 45–59.

Macneil, Ian R. 1974. "The Many Futures of Contract," *Southern California Law Review* **47**: 691–816.

March, James G., and Herbert A. Simon. 1958. *Organizations.* New York: John Wiley and Sons.

Marengo, Luigi, and Giovanni Dosi. 2005. "Division of Labor, Organizational Coordination and Market Mechanisms in Collective Problem-Solving," *Journal of Economic Behavior & Organization* **58**(2): 303–326.

Marglin, Stephen A. 1974. "What Do Bosses Do?" *Review of Radical Political Economy* **6**: 33–60.

Margolis, Stephen E. 2013. "A Tip of the Hat to Kay and QWERTY," *Research Policy* **42**(6): 1188–1190.

Marsden, Ben. 2002. *Watt's Perfect Engine: Steam and the Age of Invention.* New York: Columbia University Press.

Marx, Karl. 1961 [1887]. *Capital.* Moscow: Foreign Languages Publishing House.

Masten, Scott E. 2006. "Authority and Commitment: Why Universities, Like Legislatures, Are Not Organized as Firms," *Journal of Economics & Management Strategy* **15**(3): 649–684.

Masten, Scott E., James W. Meehan and Edward A. Snyder. 1991. "The Costs of Organization," *Journal of Law, Economics, & Organization* **7**(1): 1–25.

Masten, Scott E., and Edward A. Snyder. 1993. "*United States versus United Shoe Machinery Corporation*: On the Merits," *Journal of Law and Economics* **36**(1): 33–70.

McCloskey, Deirdre N. 1997. "The Good Old Coase Theorem and the Good Old Chicago School: A Comment on Zerbe and Medema," in Steven G. Medema, ed., *Coasean Economics: The New Institutional Economics and Law and Economics.* Dordrecht: Kluwer Academic Publishing, pp. 239–248.

McManus, John C. 1975. "The Costs of Alternative Economic Organizations," *The Canadian Journal of Economics/Revue canadienne d'Economique* **8**(3): 334–350.

Ménard, Claude. 2021. "Hybrids: Where Are We?" *Journal of Institutional Economics* **18**(2): 297–312.

Miceli, Thomas J. 2015. "Transaction-Specific Investments and Organizational Choice: A Coase-to-Coase Theory," *Journal of Institutional Economics* **11**(2): 283–299.

Miceli, Thomas J., and Kathleen Segerson. 2012. "Holdups and Holdouts: What Do They Have in Common?" *Economics Letters* **117**(1): 330–333.

Milgrom, Paul, and John Roberts. 1990. "Bargaining Costs, Influence Costs, and the Organization of Economic Activity," in James E. Alt and Kenneth A. Shepsle, eds., *Perspectives on Positive Political Economy.* New York: Cambridge University Press, pp. 57–89.

Mokyr, Joel, Chris Vickers and Nicolas L. Ziebarth. 2015. "The History of Technological Anxiety and the Future of Economic Growth: Is This Time Different?" *Journal of Economic Perspectives* **29**(3): 31–50.

Monteverde, Kirk, and David J. Teece. 1982. "Appropriable Rents and Quasi-Vertical Integration," *Journal of Law and Economics* **25**(2): 321–328.

Moss, Scott. 1984. "The History of the Theory of the Firm from Marshall to Robinson and Chamberlin: The Source of Positivism in Economics," *Economica* **51**(203): 307–318.

Nelson, Richard R. 1991. "Why Do Firms Differ, and How Does It Matter?" *Strategic Management Journal* **12**: 61–74 (Winter).

Nelson, Richard R., and Sidney G. Winter. 1982. *An Evolutionary Theory of Economic Change*. Cambridge, MA: Harvard University Press.

Nelson, Richard R., and Sidney G. Winter. 2002. "Evolutionary Theorizing in Economics," *The Journal of Economic Perspectives* **16**(2): 23–46 (Spring).

Nevins, Allan, and Frank Ernest Hill. 1962. *Ford: Decline and Rebirth, 1933–1962*. New York: Charles Scribner's Sons.

Newman, Mark E. J. 2006. "Modularity and Community Structure in Networks," *Proceedings of the National Academy of Sciences* **103**(23): 8577–8582.

North, Douglass C. 1981. *Structure and Change in Economic History*. New York: Norton.

North, Douglass C., John Joseph Wallis and Barry R. Weingast. 2009. *Violence and Social Orders: A Conceptual Framework for Interpreting Recorded Human History*. New York: Cambridge University Press.

Ostrom, Elinor. 2015. *Governing the Commons: The Evolution of Institutions for Collective Action*. New York: Cambridge University Press.

Pagano, Ugo. 2000. "Public Markets, Private Orderings and Corporate Governance," *International Review of Law and Economics* **20**: 453–477.

Parnas, David L. 1972. "On the Criteria for Decomposing Systems into Modules," *Communications of the ACM* **15**(12): 1053–1058 (December).

Parnas, David L., Paul C. Clemens and David M. Weiss. 1985. "The Modular Structure of Complex Systems," *IEEE Transactions on Software Engineering* **11**(3): 259–266 (March).

Peaucelle, Jean-Louis, and Cameron Guthrie. 2011. "How Adam Smith Found Inspiration in French Texts on Pin Making in the Eighteenth Century," *History of Economic Ideas* **19**(3): 41–68.

Penrose, Edith T. 1952. "Biological Analogies in the Theory of the Firm," *The American Economic Review* **42**(5): 804–819.

Penrose, Edith T. 1959. *The Theory of the Growth of the Firm*. Oxford: Basil Blackwell.

Pinker, Steven. 2000. *Words and Rules: The Ingredients of Language*. New York: Harper.

Pirenne, Henri. 1925. *Medieval Cities: Their Origins and the Revival of Trade*. Princeton, NJ: Princeton University Press.

Polanyi, Michael. 1958. *Personal Knowledge*. Chicago: University of Chicago Press.

Popper, Karl. 1963. *Conjectures and Refutations: The Growth of Scientific Knowledge*. London: Routledge and Kegan Paul.

Pratten, Clifford F. 1980. "The Manufacture of Pins," *Journal of Economic Literature* **18**(1): 93–96.

Raff, Daniel M. G., and Lawrence H. Summers. 1987. "Did Henry Ford Pay Efficiency Wages?" *Journal of Labor Economics* **5**(4): S57-S86.

Rashdall, Hastings. 1895. *The Universities of Europe in the Middle Ages*. Oxford: Oxford University Press, Volume 1.

Richardson, G. B. 1972. "The Organisation of Industry," *The Economic Journal* **82**(327): 883–896.

Roberts, Paul Craig, and Matthew Stephenson. 1973. *Marx's Theory of Exchange, Alienation, and Crisis.* Stanford: Hoover Institution.

Robertson, Paul L., and Lee J. Alston. 1992. "Technological Choice and the Organization of Work in Capitalist Firms," *The Economic History Review* **45**(2): 330–349.

Robinson, Joan. 1956. *The Accumulation of Capital.* Homewood, IL: Richard D. Irwin.

Rowell, David, and Luke B. Connelly. 2012. "A History of the Term 'Moral Hazard,'" *Journal of Risk and Insurance* **79**(4): 1051–1075.

Ruttan, Vernon W., and Yujiro Hayami. 1984. "Toward a Theory of Induced Institutional Change," *The Journal of Development Studies* **20**(4): 203–223.

Ruxton, Graeme D. 2002. "The Possible Fitness Benefits of Striped Coat Coloration for Zebra," *Mammal Review* **32**(4): 237–244.

Schelling, Thomas C. 1960. *The Strategy of Conflict.* Cambridge, MA: Harvard University Press.

Schelling, Thomas C. 1984. *Choice and Consequence.* Cambridge, MA: Harvard University Press.

Shackle, G. L. S. 1967. *The Years of High Theory: Invention and Tradition in Economic Thought, 1926–1939.* Cambridge: Cambridge University Press.

Shackle, G. L. S. 1970. *Epistemics and Economics.* Cambridge: Cambridge University Press.

Shiller, Robert J. 2019. *Narrative Economics: How Stories Go Viral and Drive Major Economic Events.* Princeton, NJ: Princeton University Press.

Shoemaker, Nancy. 2004. *A Strange Likeness: Becoming Red and White in Eighteenth Century North America.* New York: Oxford University Press.

Shoup, Donald. 2005. *The High Cost of Free Parking.* London: Routledge.

Silver, Morris. 1984. *Enterprise and the Scope of the Firm.* London: Martin Robertson.

Simon, Herbert A. 1951. "A Formal Theory of the Employment Relationship," *Econometrica* **19**(3): 293–305 (July).

Simon, Herbert A. 1956. "Rational Choice and the Structure of the Environment," *Psychological Review* **63**(2): 129–138.

Simon, Herbert A. 1960. "The Corporation: Will It Be Managed by Machines?" in M. L. Anshen and G. L. Bach, eds., *Management and the Corporations, 1985.* New York: McGraw-Hill, pp. 17–55.

Simon, Herbert A. 1962. "The Architecture of Complexity," *Proceedings of the American Philosophical Society* **106**(6): 467–482.

Simon, Herbert A., and Allen Newell. 1958. "Heuristic Problem Solving: The Next Advance in Operations Research," *Operations Research* **6**(1): 1–10 (January-February).

Smith, Adam. 1976 [1776]. *An Enquiry into the Nature and Causes of the Wealth of Nations.* Oxford: Clarendon Press.

Smith, Henry E. 2002. "Exclusion versus Governance: Two Strategies for Delineating Property Rights," *The Journal of Legal Studies* **31**(S2): S453-S487.

Smith, Henry E. 2012. "Property as the Law of Things," *Harvard Law Review* **125**(7): 1691–1726.

Sowell, Thomas. 1980. *Knowledge and Decisions*. New York: Basic Books.

Stinchcombe, Arthur L. 1990. *Information and Organizations*. Berkeley: University of California Press.

Syverson, Chad. 2011. "What Determines Productivity?" *Journal of Economic Literature* **49**(2): 326–365.

Taylor, Frederick Winslow. 1919. *The Principles of Scientific Management*. New York: Harper & Brothers.

Tedeschi, Bob. 2000. "A Nobel Prize-Winning Idea, Conceived in the 30's, Is a Guide for Net Business," *The New York Times*, October 2, p. C12.

Teece, David J. 1980. "Economies of Scope and the Scope of the Enterprise," *Journal of Economic Behavior & Organization* **1**(3): 223–247 (September).

Teece, David J. 1986. "Profiting from Technological Innovation: Implications for Integration, Collaboration, Licensing, and Public Policy," *Research Policy* **15**(6): 285–305.

Telser, Lester G. 1960. "Why Should Manufacturers Want Fair Trade?" *Journal of Law and Economics* **3**: 86–105.

Thompson, James D. 1967. *Organizations in Action*. New York: McGraw-Hill.

Tilly, Charles. 1985. "War Making and State Making as Organized Crime," in Theda Skocpol and Peter Evans, eds., *Bringing the State Back In*. New York: Cambridge University Press, pp. 169–191.

Tullock, Gordon. 1967. "The Welfare Costs of Tariffs, Monopolies, and Theft," *Economic Inquiry* **5**(3): 224–232.

Usselman, Steven W. 1993. "IBM and Its Imitators: Organizational Capabilities and the Emergence of the International Computer Industry," *Business and Economic History* **22**(2): 1–35.

Varian, Hal R. 2002. "If There Was a New Economy, Why Wasn't There a New Economics?" *The New York Times*, January 17, p. C1.

Veysey, Laurence R. 1965. *The Emergence of the American University*. Chicago: University of Chicago Press.

Vinge, Vernor. 1993. "The Coming Technological Singularity: How to Survive in the Post-Human Era," NASA Technical Report N94–27359.

Voltaire (François-Marie Arouet). 1759. *Candide, ou l'optimisme*. Paris: Lambert.

Weber, Max. 1978. *Economy and Society: An Outline of Interpretive Sociology*. Berkeley: University of California Press.

Wells, Harwell. 2010. "The Birth of Corporate Governance," *Seattle University Law Review* **33**(4): 1247–1292 (Summer).

Wernerfelt, Birger. 1984. "A Resource-Based View of the Firm," *Strategic Management Journal* **5**(2): 171–180.

Wilder, Laura Ingalls. 1932. *Little House in the Big Woods*. New York: Harper & Brothers.

Williamson, Oliver E. 1975. *Markets and Hierarchies: Analysis and Antitrust Implications*. New York: The Free Press.

Williamson, Oliver E. 1981. "The Economics of Organization: The Transaction Cost Approach," *The American Journal of Sociology* **87**(3): 548–577.

Williamson, Oliver E. 1983a. "Antitrust Enforcement: Where It's Been, Where It's Going," *Saint Louis University Law Journal* **27**(2): 289–314 (April).

Williamson, Oliver E. 1983b. "Credible Commitments: Using Hostages to Support Exchange," *The American Economic Review* **73**(4): 519–540.

Williamson, Oliver E. 1985. *The Economic Institutions of Capitalism*. New York: The Free Press.

Williamson, Oliver E. 1991. "Comparative Economic Organization: The Analysis of Discrete Structural Alternatives," *Administrative Science Quarterly* **36**(2): 269–296.

Williamson, Oliver E. 2009. "Opening the Black Box of Firm and Market Organization: Antitrust," in Per-Olof Bjuggren and Dennis C. Mueller, eds., *The Modern Firm, Corporate Governance and Investment*. Northampton, MA: Edward Elgar, pp. 11–42.

Winter, Sidney G. 1971. "Satisficing, Selection, and the Innovating Remnant," *The Quarterly Journal of Economics* **85**(2): 237–261.

Yates, JoAnne. 2000. "Business Use of Information and Technology During the Industrial Age," in Alfred D. Chandler Jr. and James W. Cortada, eds., *A Nation Transformed by Information: How Information Has Shaped the United States from Colonial Times to the Present*. New York: Oxford University Press, pp. 107–135.

Index

132